it Must FALL

by

Lendy Swartbooi

Foreword by Jerome September

IT MUST FALL

By Classic Age Publishing

Private Bag 138,

Braamfontein,

Johannesburg

South Africa.

For more info visit:

www.classicagepublishing.co.za

Book and Cover design by Classic Age Designs

Typesetting by Rosa Penn

Edited by Vukulu Sizwe Maphindani

ISBN: 978-0-620-71863-9

Printed and bound by Digital Action SA, Cape Town, South Africa

FOREWORD

"The single story creates stereotypes, and the problem with stereotypes is not that they are untrue, but that they are incomplete. They make one story become the only story."

- Chimamanda Ngozi Adichie

Lendy Swartbooi Thobejane writes from her experiences and as such, narrates the powerful journey of a black woman choosing to remain rooted in her Cape Flats community of Ravensmead. Hers is the story of the complex and often painful journey of a society in transition from a painful apartheid past, towards building a more inclusive future based on the values of freedom, equality and dignity. Her story is both refined and raw, it is filled with emotion yet it is also rational and objective. It is a story that navigates its way through the dynamics of race relations, gender, class and the realities facing a university graduate set on making her mark. The power of her story is in the authenticity of it, and the boldness with she narrates it.

Through her writing, she challenges the single story narrative associated with the Cape Flats, a place of ganglands, crime, and hopelessness; a place of despair and "tik" and unemployment. The Cape Flats, a charity workers dream destination. Her writing tells the tale of resilience and steadfastness, great optimism, and of dreams. Through her writing, we get a window into the world of an activist set to make a positive contribution in turning her society around, against great odds. By merely writing, she challenges the single story about black South Africans. - Jerome September.

CONTENTS

INTRODUCTION ....**VI**

CHAPTER ONE **10**
   THE AFRIKANER ROOM..10

CHAPTER TWO **18**
   IT MUST FALL MOVEMENTS..18

CHAPTER THREE 24

    INSTITUTIONAL RACISM 24

CHAPTER FOUR..**34**
   I) MY STORY..34

    II) ASSISTANT LIBRARIAN 35
    III) CHARGES 46

CHAPTER FIVE..48

   SEEK TO BE SELF SUFFICIENT..................................56

CHAPTER SIX **63**

CHAPTER SEVEN..**66**
   I) INCONSISTENCY IS HER NAME – BULLYING ME WAS
PART OF THE PLAN 75

CHAPTER 8 ....**97**
   LETTERS..97

INTRODUCTION

It was the domination of the apartheid system and white supremacy in my workplace that propelled me to radically embark on the mission of liberating myself and those that I believe should be enjoying the fruits of the land that was hard long fought for by our forefathers with blood and sweat. We, the working class spend most of our lifetime at work more than we spend at home, therefore our working conditions must be pleasant and conducive enough to live. There is a monster enemy that I would like to address in this regard. Who is the enemy? The enemy is the voice that you hear every day that whispered a long time ago saying that certain people have to hate and treat others badly based on the colour of their skin. It is the very same enemy that influence and causes wars and terrorises innocent people in many African countries, and to this day – he continues doing the same thing over and over again. We all know him in different forms and I don't care what name you call him and many have different views about this enemy. But to me, he is the enemy for his purpose is to destroy the harmony and purpose of humankind.

This book is written for those who have difficulties in the workplace. The union's door is open for you but one thing is that you must know that the day you walk through that building - be guaranteed that your life will never be the same. Your line manager will always try to make your life a living hell and constantly remind you that you are nothing but just a worker. In my case, with only 15 minutes tea break and thereafter straight to clean DVDs or CDs. *"You are going to regret challenging me, I am part of Liasa organisation and also an award winning librarian, actually the best librarian in the Western Cape"*. That's what my line manager said to me. My line manager wanted me to live in fear at work. Telling me that my days are numbered. I will leave the city of Cape Town with an empty bag. This is one form of institutional racism that I talk about later in the book.

I suffered a lot of psychological trauma. I had a hell of a time working with my line manager. At some point, it was like I was going mad. I suffered a lot of stress leading to anxiety and depression. And believe me, there is a high percentage of my people going through the same problems. A lot of times I neglected my husband and children because of the depression I had to endure. At times I would just look at my door at home and cry out of the *blue* as if someone had died. My family thought that I had gone mad just because of the conversations of work I had in my sleep. I have been in and out of Doctors and

I cannot count the medications I had to take for either the back pain for standing at work for four hours or for being stressed from the treatment I got from my line manager. Just make sure you read the rest of the book as I have explained the rest of story in the chapters.

I am not racist. I would like to believe so. In fact, I have a lot of white friends out there even more than my very own people of the colour. I have a lot of white role models and people that I look up to like Dr Catherine Hutchins at the University of Cape Town and others which I spoke in detail in my first book. I literally named one of my daughters after a very dear friend from the white race, such are people that had an impact in my life. Perhaps the reason may be that it is unpopular or unexpected that people of their race may do so. There are men and women who made their mark in business, academia and some are social and political activists from the white race. My very own publisher of my first book is a former South African, a former lecturer in one of our Universities. Moreover, he is an Afrikaans speaking and now living in the UK. He and his wife did a fantastic work on my first book and I have a good relationship with them. My marketing campaign agency as well in the UK. Simply because these people are excellent at what they are doing and I do not have issues with their racial group.

Not because of their light skin colour and straight hair as it's usually expected to be the case. Otherwise, I would have run around the country searching for a noble publisher for my first book, of my own skin colour whom in any case most were not interested in publishing my first book (except for this one of course). Don't be naive and think this is a hate speech or an insult to a particular race. Don't shy away from the real issues I highlighted in this book. So what I wrote about in here are the injustices that I have experienced and the pressing issues of the struggle for our liberation of the working class and black South Africans.

This book will certainly move you. To which direction it does, unfortunately, I cannot tell you, but what I'm sure of is that at the end you will be moved. This book will make you hate me, feel sorry for me, feel encouraged, it will raise patriotism in some of you and feel that someone spoke what you have always wanted to say. It will make you want to embark in the social, academic and political movements that emancipate in the liberation of our long oppressed compatriots. In this book, I speak of the day to day issues that the average working class

are facing, particularly in the land that was ruled by colonialism which was introduced by Europeans. I speak of my story within the City of Cape Town municipality. I speak of the institutional racism that I personally have experienced after twenty two years of democracy that was fought for in bloodshed by the forefathers and comrades that stood against white domination. It's not like I woke up and decided to write about racism. In fact, I was busy planning to write about other communal stories. But being In the City where you are made to feel and see it (racism) on day to day and if you are outspoken and patriotic like me; certainly you will be convicted to mobilise yourself and join revolutionary structures for change. Steve Biko, Walter Sisulu, Ruth first, Robert Sobukwe, Tata Madiba himself and many others who fought for our liberation struggle wanted us to enjoy the fruits of the land of our forefathers.

I wrote this book knowing and understanding that certain people become sensitive and defensive when you raise the topic - racism. Why is it easy to rise and embark on social movements and sing the same songs that say no to Xenophobia? Is it because it's black people fighting each other? Perhaps you may find me irrelevant on this one, of course, because you don't want to confront head on to this issue. As much as xenophobia exist, equally so racism exists in the Western Cape and maybe in other parts of the country. Now you will hate me on this one. But this is a dominant subject in this book. Maybe it's advisable that you stop reading because what I wrote about later in the chapters is a harsh reality without fear or intimidation and that, you may not want to read about. I speak about the issues of Transformation later in the chapters. People are of the view that by simply hiring few blacks and put them as the face of the company or organisation pressed by affirmative action and BBBEE policies means that the company or organisation is transformed. Yes, we can see the colour at the face of the company but who's at the core of decision making? Who is involved in the recruitment and operational level to ensure that there is proper implementation of those policies or structures? Or Is it a *"just scrap that nonsense and throw it in the bin."* Who is at the core of capital injection to drive your institutions because of those my friend, are the people likely to say jump and all you will need to say is how high. As I write this book, I am boiling to write about the Land Reformation issues. That topic in itself is something, perhaps I should leave it to the Zimbabwean people for they understand how Europeans and colonialism never wanted to meet Africans half way. Even today, in our country we struggle with the very same topic. I understand that you are probably thinking that I'm now out of line, go out and read what happened to the Zimbabwean nation instead of hating the Zim government and their leader.

In this book, I speak about issues around victimisation, harassment, and how grievances and disputes are handled.

Trust me, it's never in your favour. I speak of how the policies are misused and workers' rights are violated. It saddened me when you tell those that hold the highest authority about how your manager violated the policy and the response being that your manager has got his own style or way of doing things. Not at all. **I repeat - NOT at all**. In a democratic country, you don't just wake up and decide that today I will nail my employees outside organisational policies. In this book, I will be talking all about these issues and give a bonus chapter on grievance procedures and disputes, and I have given examples of how I executed my disputes. I have also highlighted the mistakes that I made and gave tips on how to go about doing it the right way.

1

THE AFRIKANER ROOM

I'm writing about this room so that you may have a clear perspective of the environment in which I was working in. precisely because I raised the issues of transformation and institutional racism. This chapter forms much of the foundation where my arguments of transformation are based on.

This room is the reflection of what is taking place at my work. This room is hidden from the public. It's the room where they kept all the information on Charles Davidson and Bell and Cecil John Rhodes. The city of Cape Town promotes racism at Bellville Library by promoting the paintings of Charles

Davidson Bell in the reference section. The main place of birth for the Afrikaners. This reference section is situated downstairs in the library - you can either take stairs or the lift. Bell was known as the Surveyor General in the Cape colony. Born in Scotland, he viewed Khoikhoi men and women as "'useless drunkards" or "lazy members of the Cape society". Charles made sure that the Khoisan people gain the reputation of being identified as "the world's most beastly people" or the "most wretched race" through his artistic work. This artistic work of the colonial artist - Charles Davidson Bell with specific reference of the Khoikhoi being despicable as habitual drunkards, social misfits and scandalous characters. Bell portrays the Khoisan women as scandalous women as well as discourteous of the worst kind. He portrayed Khoisan as "drunken good for nothing with criminal career paths". He was the one drawing them and spreading the message artistically. He successfully degraded and humiliated Black people through his artwork.

Going to this library and seeing this images on the walls made me fear the dominance of white supremacy in my own motherland. Somehow this room gives me *ghost bums*. Whenever I walked passed the door, I felt how much my hair rose from the outside as if the man (Charles) is looking and smiling at me. I, at times, thought that perhaps it is the anti-depression medication that I am taking that is playing some mind games with me. I hated that portrait of that man Davidson Charles Bell. I did not need to be alive to have met this man face to face - his demonic spirit is walking around freely in and out of Bellville Library. The library is living his dream of always thinking nothing of Khoisan people. We are always regarded as unprofessional no matter what qualification or experience we have we will remain nothing in their eyes. The chairperson of the Friends of the Library is the previous chief librarian of Bellville library this is another Afrikaner. The friends of the library are old Afrikaners. Those ones that benefited greatly from apartheid. Those ones that got their education at UCT in the 1980's and ever since are owners of massive land that was taken from my forefathers by force. This land was never given back or shared for that matter but the issue will never be discussed at work. All they will say how they despise Winnie Mandela she has done so money wrongs things during apartheid I have asked these white people what about the murdering of black people that they forefathers have done. Then all of a sudden our conversation is over.

Outside the room is the pictures and painted portraits of the

man himself just outside the door. This man is very famous for painting incentive portraits of the Khoisan. This is the secret room of Bellville Library. In no other library, you will find a room in the city of Cape Town where they have a *secret room*.

You need permission from the librarian for you to enter the room. No member of the public is allowed inside that specific room because according to management, the information that is kept there is highly sentimental and valuable. On the door of the room is a note which says *"collections"*. I got inside that room in 2014. In this room, the first thing you see is the old emblem of the **Bellville Library Municipality** when it was still managed by the Afrikaner people - the Afrikaans-speaking white people. Bellville Library had its own municipality and was the library that benefited greatly from the apartheid regime. The friends of the library also play an important role and will never want a black person from a previously marginalised community because then it means this person will expose this *Afrikaner room* and it will be demolished. How can the city of Cape Town allow a room in a public library dedicated to colonialism? There will never be change at Bellville Library as long as the Afrikaner room exists inside the library that firmly believes in the norms and culture of the colonialist, Charles Davidson Bell. There is a huge cry at this library for internal transformation. This library still holds on to the horrid information of the past. Again, I asked black people who works there, that how can they be content with the fact that there is an Afrikaner room that promotes institutional racism, discrimination and victimisation? They replied – it's easy. If your brand new car is being deducted from your salary you will not say anything. If you only have grade 12, you will be silent forever. This made it worse for me, I could no longer breathe in this space that promotes racism to the highest possible way. That's why the line manager, the management and all white people employed at this place will never see blacks as equals; whether you have graduated from a world class university like myself - all that made me consciously aware that these things, from apartheid, are still very alive. The city of Cape Town needs to change the power structures of this place. Then again, this is the city of Cape Town's hiding place. They will not change it - the rooms belong to the DA political party in the Western Cape and I say so for it is a governing party in this place.

Again, I have asked those who have worked there for more than five years, that how can they be satisfied with the fact that there is a room called *Die Afrikaner room*. The answer I got from my colleagues was, "we have houses and cars that are debited from our salaries which we get from the city of Cape Town, therefore we will not challenge them because they have top notch lawyers and will make sure that you get thrown out of the city of Cape town for good." I made a mental note of those words. But then again, people have died for us so that we cannot only have the freedom to walk wherever we want to but be equal in our workplace. One should not be above the other just because the one is lighter than the other one. I had taken out a massive loan and need a job to be able to pay it every month but I cannot be content at all. Even if I lose my job, at least I can sleep peacefully knowing that I have done my part and break the silence but can you sleep and suffer in silence just because of the general status quo you have to uphold in the community? Deep down you are living in fear. I am convicted of leaving you with this questions. If this room does not promote institutional racism and enforcing a sense of inferiority among black people, then why is it not open to the public but always locked? Secondly, why is it only former apartheid regime fellows, the so-called "white Afrikaners" allowed to visit this room in the name of that they are friends of the library? That to me seems like a ritual performing shrine. And lastly, why is me, as a descendant of the Khoi-nation woman has to be monitored during training as to what to touch and what not to in my very own working environment? This is not a private institution, it is a public institution funded by the taxes of our very own people who are exploited harshly in their working environment. Like I said, you may not like my views, but I continue to bring this type of questions forth in continuing the emancipatory programme of the freedom of the working class. I don't mind being crucified for exposing injustices for our long oppressed people of the land. I have been an activist as I said this whilst at school, at Varsity, in my acting career and now in my working environment. Of course, I don't mind having lost a lot of friends along the way and believe me, at times I had to fly solo. At least I'm telling my story and the more of us open up without fear and intimidation and fight for the liberation of our struggle, the more we can overcome our enemy. Irrespective of what level of governance we hold or level of the ladder from the tea lady to top executive positions may be in our working environment, we need to speak up! If we exhaust proper channels then that way, we may have a transformation which I will be speaking about later in the next chapters.

Friends of the Library are in another form the donors of the library with the aim to help the functionality of the library. I, therefore, was convinced that this is exactly the white monopoly capital that our trade unionists have been talking about and of course, they got crucified for it. The system is monopolised that "If you keep our apartheid legacy then we will keep you alive and if you don't, we pull out our Resources. Meaning, keep our *Afrikaner room* and we will keep on letting the money rolling in for the library. This is exactly what the

Europeans are doing to African countries. We all know that the countries that are not complying with these tactics get punished. Our very own neighbours – The Zimbabwean nation can tell the story very well. Trust me, these people are very wealthy fellas.

One day I was very shocked as I was with my Xhosa speaking colleague. A patron came and spoke in Afrikaans. She was of a view that I cannot speak Afrikaans. Of course, at most instances, I pretended not to know the language. These were her words, "this is an Afrikaans Library, it has an Afrikaans language policy and she needs an Afrikaans speaking person that she can speak to." We referred her to the Senior Librarian. This matter was raised at the meeting by my colleague and the line manager pretended to know nothing about the matter. My question was, how can a patron talk about the Afrikaans language policy that I knew nothing about and the senior staff did not correct her about it? She knew what she was talking about because that's how the library was instituted long before we worked there and this has not changed after we attained democracy. This was an insult for the non-Afrikaans speaking in their place of work and land of birth. Again, I wrote about my struggle, I raised my experiences and points of view, I therefore leave you and politicians to judge. You must not forget *the* *Afrikaner* *room.***

2

IT MUST FALL MOVEMENTS

The #itMustFall was born not only of the struggle that we, the working class and the majority of the people of SA experiences, but also at the time when our country is having riots like #feemustfall, #Rhodesmustfall and the #zumamustfall. #mustfall represented the same struggle. It has been twenty two years of democracy and a lot has not much changed. The #itmustfall uprisings and movements have been demonstrations of how unequal societal South Africa is. A lot of people, when these movements were formulated, had various negative thoughts around these formations. Some said that students are lazy and "Toitoi" because they are failing their university courses. Others said that statues need not be touched as they represent the history of the so called their "ancestors". The reality is that these movements were born out of the continuous struggle of freedom which was theoretically obtained when Tata was released. But in reality, that freedom is no way found anywhere in our dispensation. It is still the Ideal. I don't deny the fantastic policies around this issues of freeness. In practice, we would see our people flourishing, our educational system enhancing and incapacitating our people to create jobs for themselves. Perhaps enabling the spirit of entrepreneurship amongst our youth. Thus enhancing the improvement of our economic freedom.

It's amazing, well common to some extent, that when you challenge the higher authority as a Black woman - your academic credentials begin to be challenged or questioned. I was not surprised when I was asked if I had completed my studies. It was awkward because, for my case, it had nothing to do with my qualifications. Anyway, that I'll leave for later in the book where I explain and demonstrate all that in detail. That's how Europeans thought/think of us. Those were Charles Bell's core beliefs as I wrote earlier in the book that black people are mount to nothing.

In my opinion, these are the movements we need to encourage more in order to achieve economic freedom and emancipation in the struggle for our liberation. Simply because most of these students are young and vibrant. Believe me, we need our elders in guiding us to move forward and tell the history of the birth of our struggles. But that will not be enough as the majority of these fellows are deeply institutionalised.

Let me tell you something. White people living in this day, won't come to you and tell you how ugly and *monkey-like* you may be. That is out of fashion and of course, it can get someone arrested and we all know it. But they will create a system and an environment in which you will feel their presence. Go to all the itMustFall movements and search for the core issues that are at the head of birth to such movements and trust me, racism and apartheid legacies are at the centre. This is a disease that got to most of them. A study was done in some country some time ago. There was a large group of people in a refugee camp. These people were struggling. Life was hard for them and amongst them was one white person. Everyone was concerned about their hardships and when they asked the only Whiteman who was amongst them about his wariness. He was not worried about the struggle. He was just glad on the fact that he is better than the rest. In what way I cannot say. But many times these kind of stories are real. You might be working with one, having the same Job description and title. But they would regard themselves better than you. If you haven't experienced it in this country, then you probably live in the Ideal South Africa of Mandela and what shall we say? - well for you. Because we all wish to live in that kind of environment. Personally, I have encountered the hardest ones (White people). Perhaps it's better in other countries which we most dream we could go live in such places. In search of greener pastures there, at least I would like to believe. Let me tell you. You will see Coloureds and Africans turning against one another. I'm starting to see that happening in Cape Town. Whose idea is it that someone is better than the other? The reality is that white people have capital and Africans have the political will. When you talk about "statues" - Xenophobia arises. When you talk about racism - the focus is on the Guptas. When we say that the land must be returned - people unite themselves through the Zuma must fall campaign. Be careful and look at the trends and study what I'm saying carefully. Most of us like to go where the wind blows (especially black people). Even when the wind is propelled by artificial generators. Stats tells that issues around racism and white supremacy never really get that far. Why? I leave it for you to think about it. The UCT Rhodesmustfall movement has done it. Those students stood their ground and Rhodes have fallen. Now their mandate is to tackle the policies. Perhaps one day someone will say Charles Bell and his principles must fall at Bellville Library.

I recall back in my days at varsity. I have touched a little similar scenarios in my first book **Boonkie in the community**. I remember doing a course called voice. I grew up speaking Afrikaans. Perhaps I should say Afrikaps. Because the kind of Afrikaans I speak and most Cape Coloureds speak is not that Wynberg Girls high type of language. But a little mixed with its own accent. I did all my subjects in Afrikaans and you can imagine how poor my academic English. My lecturer wanted me to speak my poor English with a European accent. I was told that I won't be able to survive my lecturers with the way I kept going. I argued this because remember, I am a Capetonian and a South African. I could not have changed and became European. This is a kind of a problem that our people faces in higher institutions of learning. I had a friend who was in the same class with me. She was sent to the hospital for an operation for her throat because she was sounding "funny" according to the lecturers. This is a form of discrimination and it manifests in the form of racism many times. When I begin my acting career I enrolled with an agency. After a while, I was removed from their books because they could not find a job for me because of my accent. Their reason was that most jobs required at least some European or American accent. It is still happening today that in theatre play people will tell you that there no work for cape accent.

On this note, I would like to leave you with this thought. If you look into the Johannesburg Stock Exchange you will realise that yes indeed - our country is far from transforming. Over ninety two percent of the population comprises of black people including coloureds and Indians. Ninety plus a percentage of listed companies are white owned companies. Look at the proportionality of black people and this proportionality of wealth distribution and tell me that we are transformed. Again, white people own a bigger proportion of the land. Do we have economic freedom? And yet when you talk about white supremacy and racism you seem to be insane. Which leads me into the next topic in the next chapter.

3

INSTITUTIONAL RACISM

English is not my first language, and I'm not intending to make it one. So my explanation of racism may not be like of an English man who wrote the Oxford dictionary somewhere in Britain. But my understanding of racism is that it is when people tyrannise one another based on the colour of their skin, mainly from different races. I am explaining this because a lot of people freak out when you mention the word racism. It is surprising that when you talk about xenophobia black people, in particular, are not offended but join and embark in joining the movements that eradicate this sick tendency. I refer to black people because when you say xenophobia we look into the black townships in which our Africans find it easy to settle and associate. Of course, those are the legacies of the apartheid regime and particularly – colonialism as a whole. I should believe that if they were able to associate with the rich white suburbans we would see a similar scenario. Black people are not offended about the topic because we understand that it is not all that are Xenophobic. Therefore we need not to be apologetic and fearful when we speak about racism - and white people must stop feeling sorry and feel that this average township girl have nothing to contribute but resounding on attacking us. A wise man once said; "There is yes, a tendency that - the majority of whites want us to stop talking about racism but they themselves do nothing about stopping themselves from being racists".

There was one vibrant young lady who once wrote and addressed black and white people on social media. She received a lot of comments which the majority of those came from the white community who applauded her. She wrote a good article and white people felt that she needed to be voted for as a president of this country. I personally liked her article but had one problem with it. In her address to black people, she mentioned that we need to stop complaining and blaming the apartheid system and start doing something for ourselves. To the white community, she said that they must forget about dreaming of how nice it is in the UK and Australia and come on board. I agree, fully so. My only problem is that Most people want to feel validated and feel that they are at home. Well, I guess that's just part of our human nature. How do you go about that when the legacy of apartheid practices are thrown at you in your everyday life? You are certainly bound to remember the legacy that brought the subject of the matter. We don't want to talk much about the past. We want to do things for ourselves. But how do you go about achieving that when these are still factors arising from the past that inhibits you? Maybe psychologists can give us an answer. But that answer must be politicised because without a radical political formation we will forever be inhibited. This is not a hate speech or an article of hate - but my struggle of a democratic dispensation.

Our fellow comrades and colleagues out there are made to believe that certain things are and can be achieved by those who oppress them. White monopoly capital is a system made similar to the apartheid regime to manipulate our people not to see the potential that is in themselves and also not to utilise their very own recourses for the betterment of their own communities. In fact, in most cases, the two work parallel to each other. White supremacy is mushrooming more and more. As I'm writing this book, I read a paper where somewhere in

Joburg, white people are intimidating blacks with their former apartheid flag. There was a story written that some senior bosses are wearing apartheid T-shirts under their jackets and when they are in their offices they take off such jackets. Even when they conduct interviews, they put on such attire. This is the kind of intimidation I experienced as I wrote about *in the Afrikaner room* chapter earlier in the book. This is an institutionalised system of a kind, the oppressor is trying to again dominate the territory.

A lot of people are being denied access or privileges as others in their working environment as it was in my case based on the colour of one's skin. We are made to believe that we cannot fit in other sectors of our work. Let alone the qualifications and experiences you may have, just the fact that you are of a particular race you are denied those privileges. It became difficult for my oppressor to believe how a Khoisan descent published a book in the UK. Certainly not. It became clear when my boss said to me that I need to give freely my book to her and she will review it first if it fits to be placed at the library. That is institutional racism. I have seen expensive books bought in bulks without being reviewed just because a white patron recommend it. When white authors are brought to our disposal they must be worshipped. But for blacks, the first thing you argue is that it's not a book but some poems, then investigate if it's really you who indeed wrote it. I had a very stupid argument with my line manager when she told me it is not a book but Kindle. How can you in the first place have a Kindle if you did not write something? For someone with a degree relating to books and many years of service in the library. To me, that was simply clear of how white people view us. I was not surprised later when a German fella told me that my book is not needed at the library because it was poorly written.

Our people are made to believe that they are mounted to nothing. If there was a management meeting from the director or district for line managers, we are being given only certain minutes of the meeting. It is only certain information, not all that we are supposed to know. Perhaps in their thoughts is that if we were to know what the city is planning or putting in place we would become better and clever. This is exactly what has been happening back in apartheid. I'm talking about institutional racism. It is evident when you compare the notes we receive and the ones of other districts or worse when there are opportunities given to people to participate if they have interest and you only hear about it when the closing date has passed. When I wanted to participate in the Amabookies reading competition, I was denied the opportunity to do so because *people did not know me.* Yes, that's the reason my line manager gave to me.

Since I started at work - I was told that I am on training. I was then in training for a very long time. There was no plan of what it was about and how long I will be on it. I could never function in other areas as I was in this unstructured training. The aim was to Corner me so that I cannot develop and grow to function anywhere. My colleagues were made to believe that I cannot perform even simple duties and hence I remained on training that I did not have deadlines or monitoring and evaluation plan for anything.

My colleagues were terrified to be seen talking to me because it would be believed that they are fighting the same struggle as me and therefore would be victimised. When I went on to put my grievance level 3 I became a soldier of the working class. It was very clear that I embark on a revolutionary and radical process of my working conditions. I was at all times wearing my SAMWU union T-shirt. A red one. If you live in my country or read about it. You'll understand what sort of people wear red T-shirts and talk revolutionary language without fear. Perhaps back in the days since we happen to see cheap politicking these days. It is unpopular to see members of trade unions wearing their union gear for a simple reason that they would be seen to be against the oppressor, therefore victimised. That is institutional racism.

Colleagues of the race would even go miles to spy on you and stab you at the back. I was stabbed so many times by the people that I trusted most in my own work. People went miles to give me lifts and buy me things with the plan of giving back information to my boss about my life and plans. I realised that soon enough and in no time, I knew that they were reporting back. Just because they needed approval from the boss and some, they literally told me that they would suck up and not get in any wrong books with the boss so they may get promotion and a good reference. I'm not saying that people must go around fighting with their bosses because they are white. No no no no. As a matter of fact, there are very good bosses out there. If they had advertised themselves we would have all been on a queue to apply to work under them. Maybe those who eager to work for boss. But sucking up for the sake of approval or reference that is being institutionalised. If we can work hard and with fairness based on what our constitution preaches - then we certainly can achieve greater heights.

Racism has evolved in today's life. Don't be fooled by

modernization and big English words popped out of the dictionary to call things or classifies them. In the 70s, you knew racism when a white man pointed at you with a gun, beating you or when called the K... word.

Today you know it when you and the person of a different race, mostly the white race have the same job description and not doing the same thing, same qualifications and experience or you even have a better one but denied promotion but the other one gets it because of their privileged skin, having a qualification applying for an internal post and getting rejected but someone outside gets, volunteers for free while other whites get paid a stipend. Don't ask me for proof because you will be shocked. I know my story very well. I'm not naive nor trying to fetch points and make the book look good. Yes, there are white people that even without qualifications are brilliant in what they are doing. You also have black people with big qualifications but lazy as hell - I personally encountered a few. But here I'm talking about pure discrimination based on the colour of one's skin.

Today, it is still applicable in the Western Cape that certain areas are clustered with white people as compared to others. I'm not talking about apartheid inheritance here. I'm talking about mere closed doors. When you phone an agency looking for accommodation, they first listen to your accent then you are told that the flat or the house has been taken. But come a month later it's still available. I recently read a story here in Cape Town where a black couple went to view a place and were told that it's taken. On their way out there was a white couple coming to view the same place and were given an opportunity. Perhaps those blacks had an American accent to have even got an opportunity to come this far to view the place and discovered that they are actually blacks. But this is common. I'm talking about being institutionalised. Certain areas belong to a certain group of few European individuals. Same thing about schools. You all know this. I cannot even begin. You'll hear people saying you don't stay in this area so you children must go to the very township you come from. How would you even ever take your children to good schools when you cannot even move into those areas for accommodation? When I was trying to enrol my children to one of the good white school. I went there on the first day of February on their opening. They told me that they will start mid-February then I can register them for the following year. I then went back at the time given and was told that actually, they are not taking kids from outside their school. Can you believe it? But that is very real. Let me leave you with this one. Black people in Joburg and elsewhere in the country are prospering academically, businesswise, and their lives are better off. There is an influx of white people into the Western

Cape region. Why?

4

MY STORY

I Reported a child molestation case in 2012 when I was volunteering for two years. I was even dragged out of the library when the senior librarian called a police officer to chuck me out. It was because I reported this matter to District 5. I even reported this matter and took one of ladies that was badly molested to our Counsellors' house. If you read **Boonkie in the community** (My first book) you'll understand that the issues around women and children abuse are very closest to my heart. I have been much of an activist around this topic and I did not compromise when I reported the matter. It was this matter that put me in all this drama. And that's where it began. The district manager did not handle the matter in an appropriate manner. She instead attacked me around this issue where she started accusing me of my behaviour around the libraries she manages - you will see that on the email indicated at the back of the book.

II) ASSISTANT LIBRARIAN

In order for you to understand what is taking place in this is you must read the book *Boonkie in the Community* especially the five-hour worker. There is a picture there of a similar incidence. Bellville Library is the only library where there is a huge difference between a part time worker and full-time worker as they say. Part-time workers in the City I work in my case works five hours while full-timers work eight hours daily. But the job description is the same. A black five hour like myself does not get a bonus. You have to let the city deduct an amount with the system called Tax smoothing bonus from your salary every month. Most white people were paid 10% more than most black people then again this only happens in the Western Cape. When it comes to running a programme - you must forget about i

I was told that you need to have a degree in order to run programmes by the district manager but there was a library under the supervision of the very same manager that had a white person running the library as a senior librarian. Prior to this position, she was employed as a children librarian without a degree. Just the fact that she was white. I strongly emphasise this because I had not seen any black person employed in this form and holding such a position without proper qualifications, perhaps you are reading this and you have someone in mind, maybe that will help but does not mean this type of corruption is exempted. I was very much shocked when I questioned and brought a witness at CCMA that *why are white women employed without a degree?* And I was told that the HR has made a mistake. Can you believe it? When you questions the integrity of such governance, it is simply a mistake. Are whites untouchable? Remember, this is not some European guy's company who can simply do as he please. This is the government of the **African people**.

Five hour workers in other Libraries are the ones organising reading programmes but at Bellville Library, a five hour worker or an assistant librarian is seen as an unprofessional. Moreover, there is a lady that is doing the chess club at the library but have no library science degree, in addition, she's a volunteer at the library. Why is that? When I was in grievance level three, the executive director gave an example which I find ridiculous. She said that in bigger settings like hospitals a general practitioner performs one task whereas in smaller hospitals they perform even to the level of theatre tasks, true, but irrelevant in this case. If it was the case then why do the library go out and hire unprofessional people to help in running the programmes whereas there are qualified people employed. In my case, I am a trained professional story teller and I write my own poems. Instead of using myself or other black staff they'd rather go and hire a white person who did not even know Jack or what she was doing. Black people worked at the circulation desk like slaves at my workplace. This is the institutional racism that I spoke about earlier. There were no chairs for us to sit on at the circulation desk. I became vocal about it and was starting to develop a back problem which put me in and out of doctors. Just standing for four hours with a 15-minute tea break then back on your feet. You are either shelving books for an hour, making a display or like me - cleaning 100 DVDs for that remaining hour. if you don't, you will then be called in by the senior librarian that you are not meeting the cleaning target of the library while the other white assistant librarians are having a fantastic time taking a snack break at the desk or looking through their window at the people sitting on the part and talking about how many properties they have accumulated.

There was a Senior Librarian who did a research on public libraries for her master thesis before I came into my working place. In her report, she was echoing that people are suffering at a certain library but no one pays any attention. If you do ask for a bursary to further your development within the library I was told that I am lucky number 10, on the waiting list for the bursaries. When I ask *why must I wait for 10 years to study because of operational services.* I failed to understand the city in this regard. Because there were people earning fat salaries that they benefited from back in apartheid but still get bursaries which pay for their fees. I understand that there are those who gained or inherited from apartheid in the new democracy - the government cannot come and cut those salaries and privileges. But equally so those who were disadvantaged ought to be prioritised when it comes to government funding. The closest example would be the student financial Aid. Most of us started with low salaries but it's even more difficult to access the City 's funding and told that you can pay for your own studies. In a new democracy, it is not a privilege but my right to access funds to study. But this process is facilitated by line managers and if you, like in my case you are in wrong terms with yours (line manager) will never see the light of it. How can black people be educated and take over while we sit and watch? - I thought.

Part time assistant librarians like myself who were employed after 2012 were employed on the city's new Total Cost of Employment known as TCEO. This simply meant that you are starting on a very low scale. Your salary would roughly be R6000, and after deductions, you will get R5000 as compared to your other colleagues who are having the same job description but have started with a salary of R10000 with full bonuses on the 27th of November every year. I was the lowest paid part time assistant librarian at work. I was employed on the condition that *if you do want a bonus, you must contact the Human Resource (HR) and ask to have a bonus in November then they will scan and email you the form that you must fill and send it back*. This, however, will be to your detriment because you must know one thing - that the city of Cape Town will take more than R500 every month from your salary and not give it back to you. Another painful thing was that if you email them and ask them that you no longer wants a tax smoothing done on your form you will never get your money back and that's what I have experienced.

As I have mentioned earlier, I suffered from depression from the day I got employed (2 September 2013) in the city of Cape Town until throughout. My life got worse when I had to attend the grievance hearing on April 2015 in Maitland head office of

LSI (Library Science and Information) against my line manager. I was the least paid employee at work but it did not stop me from speaking the truth. There is a perception that the only people that are entitled to take on and speak about issues that expose the injustices can only be those who are having fat salaries. Well, simply because maybe they have enough savings or they automatically qualifies to be vocal based on their economic status. I came to differ with that. My colleagues at work thought that I was gone mad because I was very vocal about the vindictive situation at work and even told me that "you cannot take on the City of Cape Town by yourself." I was told that I will never move out of poverty because I want to speak out against racism. "Good luck," they said. Some even laughed at me while they were also suffering in silence. As I'm writing this book, there are a lot of people going through the same thing that I went through. Let me give you methods that you can use to investigate this. Take an evaluation form and ask employees to fill it anonymously indicating if they are happy in their workplace and indicate the reasons why they say so. Especially in the Western Cape region. You'll then understand what I'm talking about. These workers will talk about racism at work when we are on our way to catch public transport to go home, other than that, at work they are all quiet - just pretending to be happy and contend with the current situation. When you know what the truth is and can read and understand the policies of the city of Cape Town, you do not need any support from your colleagues. Of course, you may need spiritual support for your wellbeing.

A lot of us meant nothing to the city of Cape Town. Like I said, the only reason I believe that the city employed the majority of black people is because of their past. Simply because you were previously disadvantaged but in their eyes, you are just a number employed because of their need to balance their proportionality. In my uncountable meetings with the city officials and my line manager - it became clear. In many meetings with my line manager, I just had to listen to the woman and how she did a stand-up comedy show for me and I did not even pay any fee for her performance – she performed free of charge. I thought I am really a special person to her. I was the only one in most meetings in her office. It made me feel extra special, well somehow it has. She was really trying to scare me using all sorts of tactics, instead, she made me more aware of her and made me read the policies of the city of Cape Town again and again up to a certain extent that I had to memorizes the policies out of my head so that I am very clear on how I conduct myself at work and stay out of trouble. At least in most cases. My line manager wanted me to live in fear at work. Telling me that my days are numbered. This is how our former comrades have been manipulated by the apartheid government. "You will leave the city of Cape Town with an empty bag" she said. My line manager will call me in her office and ask me to sit down and then start entertaining me with her poetry, "Lendy you have no idea who you are dealing with, you came in the city of Cape Town with an empty bag and I will make sure you will leave with an empty bag. Trust me, I thought she would make such a good comedian really. I asked if she is talking to one of her domestic workers at home. She asked me to please leave her office. But whatever she said I made sure I made a mental note of it. When I had time whilst working at the desk, I would email her words to my email. She told me that the place I am currently renting is hell wholeheartedly and that is where I will be staying for the rest of my life. She has never been to my shack but one of the ladies I worked with forced herself to visit me at my house.

Most employees are paying trade unions every month and are afraid to use them in times where they have problems at work. Most are donating to unions and suffering in pain and silence. With the fear that their Financed cars and bond houses get deducted from the same salaries and if they get dismissed what else will they do. To my brothers and sisters that have gone through suffering and into depression for months and years. I have been there where you take leave to go on holiday but you just keep on crying for days for the pain to go away. The pain will not go away but you cannot fight the city of Cape Town by yourself. Of course, you can't. You must be armed with what I call "shotguns". At night I had to visit other members of various political forms for advice. It was hell. I kept on talking to myself saying the same words over and over again. Some people thought that because I studied theatre and performing arts I'm busy with rehearsals and perhaps busy learning my lines but had no idea I'm living on anti-depressed medication. There was no rehearsal, I was going through severe depression leading to anxiety as I mentioned earlier. Some of you know what I'm talking about. My husband and my family doctor were the only ones who knew what was going on in my head. Therefore my doctor made sure he gave me a referral to see a psychologist. Because I was literally shaking. I could not keep my head still and if my head is moving I could not keep my legs still. Some in the community thought that I receive money from the previous book that I had published and had drawn into drugs and some even asked me what kind of drugs I am taking. I just said these ones are hardcore ones I am on. If they want one to be addicted like me they must first get employed by the city of Cape Town and then report racism. The person I was talking to did not hear properly and said yes - you people who work for the city of Cape town earns a lot of money every month and do not know what to do with the money instead you buy a lot of alcohol or a lot of houses. I had no choice but to smile.

These are common symptoms for people going through depression. When I was temporarily moved to the other library, I met a lady who was working for the city for twenty years. She has suffered from stress for many of those years. She had a hectic time with her line manager who put her through hell. She had a mild stroke on one side of her body. She was going through pain and these part was not functioning properly. The first thing I said to her has put a grievance against you line manager. She replied saying that she is waiting to get money for her twenty years of service. Really? I thought by the time you receive that money you won't even be knowing your own name. As I write this book I'm only a year and nine months, almost two years working for the City and with this kind of treatment certainly, I won't survive twenty years. A lot of people, it's amazing that they have the same type of thinking. Many of our forefathers have suffered these lifestyle diseases and sicknesses. Some of you as you read you have a problem with your back because the kind of chairs you are using are not proper or they did not even pass the bureau of standards. There is a song that says "ke di fongkong". I have an uncle who is suffering from a back problem for being in the truck industry for many years. Sometimes he had to drive straight two weeks with little sleep in-between. That was what apartheid did to them. By the time you retire, you cannot enjoy the little money that you worked for if there is any to begin because you are technically a scrap of a person.

III) CHARGES

When Nelson Mandela, Walter Sisulu, Ahmed kathrada and other fellow comrades became vocal about issues of racism and white supremacy they were charged. This is the system of apartheid. It manifests itself many times when you have disputes against people and they dig all the faults you have committed. It has caused an ideal and modernised way to behave even for our people. This is purely not African. I am of a view that our people when they had disputes before European colonisation, they simply would settle their matter with the king and deal with each matter as they arise individually.

It is the very same system of apartheid that when you become vocal about certain issues concerning the colonial system, you get charged. Everybody knows. When I was talking and challenging these issues with my colleagues at work I was told that the City will come after you. How did they know and who is the City? It is because the system has not changed and that was adopted from colonialists. And everyone knew about it because it was without saying that matters are handled in that manner. Let alone how ridiculous the charges themselves were. I was charged the day I spoke about white supremacy and escalated to level 3 (the city manager and mayor). Eventually, that's what I was fighting for. This is a colonial system or way to silence me or make me back off if I should put it that way. If they had their way I would have probably been killed. Of course, I say so because that's what was happening in the past. Comrade Steve Biko was a victim of such. We all know stories of many fighters of the struggle against exploitation. I was charged for emailing the counsellor, published a book, doing motivational speaking and doing private work. Yes as ridiculous as they were, but those were the charges.

5

I was shocked when one of my former colleagues told me that after I had put my grievance level three, they had a massive meeting in which HR and management were available. The purpose was to investigate the issues I have raised, mainly racism. Perhaps you may have a different opinion about this.

Racism and white supremacy will not end in the Western Cape. Unless we have a radical political will to root out such tendencies. You will hear people saying "yes political leaders must not interfere with the municipal administration." I partially agree with this, because we need a clean running of administration than having political interests waving the flag.

But it is this very reason why it will not end. Because if you have a corrupt system then it shall be so and whoever challenges the system gets crucified. I chose the word corrupt because how do you charge someone when they raise issues that require your attention. The system is setup and whoever is new comes in gets baptised. But as for me, I refused to be baptised and conforming into such a system

I was one day charting to my community members. I realised how much these people are being institutionalised. They told me that not ever in their time they have ever seen black people flogging to Cape Town. They are convinced that the DA is fighting for coloured people over this matter. They believe that black people are taking over and when you have black surnames, you are, therefore, surely guaranteed to have a job. One of them mentioned that her family relative who has a black surname was called for an interview after applying for a post. She did not get a job because they realised that she had a light skin, meaning she was coloured. It amazes me of how people would think like that. They said to me sweetie since you have a black surname you should go for this opportunity because you also look like black. Black (African) people comprise almost eighty percent of the population in the country. You certainly guaranteed to see them in the African land and that has nothing to do with affirmative action. That is how politicians' brainwashed most coloured people with such stupid thinking. I strongly believe that it is the right of the Khoisan and African people to benefit as the first priority for the land and its mineral resources. Any politicians who do not have an interest in black people and getting back their land in the vocabularies of their politicking, in my view it is institutional racism. No wonder a few years ago, madam DA herself called black people in Khayelitsha refugees. Those were simply South African people of Eastern Cape rightfully exploring the land of their ancestors.   Are   you   still   surprised?

TO NOTE:

When I was busy visiting lawyers for advice, I met a couple of people having work related cases. One man had a problem with his boss. She was overloading him with work and always giving him a hard time. He has been working there for over thirty years. He's been working close to the boss and has been sharing with him all the dirty tricks she's been doing to people. She would say to him when a new employee challenges her. She would tell him words like, "just watch that one. Give him three months and he will be out". When she hires a person for a new post. She would have a private investigator to check for where you are staying, the house you live in and everything about your family. If you have a child, when you buy a car or house then she would strike and start giving you a lot of work.

This is done because she knows that you cannot fight her as you have too many obligations onto your salary. Well, I thought to myself this man must have been working with this white lady to take his own people out and now it's his turn. Certainly, this behaviour is common in most working environments. I believe that most of you reading this can relate as well. It is embedded in the majority of white fellows to remain supreme. Most do not want black people to flourish. If you tell them at work about you Husband or wife's progress you, therefore, becomes a threat to them. Whether it's graduating from varsity or simply getting a new promotional position it's a problem. I once had an argument with some fellow white colleagues about my husband finishing his Mathematics degree. A lot could not believe that yes a black person can really graduate from such career field. Of course, you may remember that these were the courses reserved for the whites only during apartheid. He was in his final year BSc Math degree. Those are one of the highly scarce skills courses and you have to be mathematically intelligent to get to the extent of measuring with them. And that's what they had a problem with. We are viewed as monkeys as Penny Sparrow once said and with a lack of intelligence. The progress of black communities becomes a huge threat to whites.

My husband met a man once in a train. He was going to attend a court case. He worked for a white farm owner for over thirty years. He once asked his boss to help him with finance so that he can buy a car. His boss gave him all sorts of excuses about lending him some money. Eventually, this poor fellow managed to save some money and bought himself a car. He arrived at work with his new car and the white boss asked him; are you the boss now? You are now driving like one. Later the boss borrowed his car for work purpose and gave to another man to drive. It was not long the car was broken. When this poor man asked where is my car he was told that it's at the Mechanic. Three months later the car was still at Mechanic. So now this man opened a case against his boss for the car that is nowhere to be found.

Like I said, a lot of people invest their personal life in their colleagues at work and bosses. Why does it? They are mostly hoping that if they become open, people will sympathise with them and be more understanding. Let me tell you, my friend, that is the beginning of you sinking. Surprisingly why does your boss never discusses much of their personal life with you? Because you may have something to hold him or her on. They keep you not knowing what they have or not. Do you even get invited to your boss's house at some stage in your life? It may sound irrelevant to you. But I gave this I thorough thought.

I had a college friend who had problems with her husband. The husband was abusing her. They had one child together. This man was using drugs and was really not working. I mean he did not have a proper job. Everyone new about this story. I looked at her behaviour at work and I realised that she was sucking up to white people. If people know your story like that you become vulnerable to bad treatment. You can't even begin to question or challenge your boss because he or she will just give you your medicine. I had another friend who had a bipolar related problem. When she was suffering from racism at work. It was hard for her to challenge the system because her fellow colleagues knew her conditions. She could not even begin because it will just amount to just she's got a mental problem. Don't get me wrong. I'm not perpetuating bad relationships for people and their bosses. But I'm saying that the hole you are digging is not for anyone but yourself. Like the gentlemen, I discussed earlier, the one who was sabotaging his own colleagues. His boss gathered information about him and now and she's giving him hard time. Perhaps you are reading this book and thinking that these stories in my surrounding or country are not happening. But what I have written here, like I said it's my reality. I believe that a lot of South Africans especially in the Western Cape will tell you that this a reality today. Racism is still big.

Recently we had a massive media talk about all sorts of racial discrimination I had to learn and master the secret. My strong point was that I did not underestimate the city. I knew what they were capable of and how they were planning to tackle me. Their weakness was that they underestimated me. They viewed me as a low wage player. I was in no form to take them on. Little did they know that I mastered the game that they were playing. The rule is to let go of your Job. I don't mean that you must resign. But understand and make peace with the fact that they are coming after your job. Once you let go of that then you have mastered their game. Of course, it will cost you a bid. It cost me a lot. I nearly lost my mind at some stage. But device means to counteract this. I knew I'm a writer. I will then make a living out of my writing. Perhaps when you read this book hopefully you have bought it then I should have made enough money to go on with life. Well, the reality is that I needed to write this story to help those who can relate to my story and are seeking advice and a way out of their misery. The only thing the city had on me was my job that's it. I had a range of options once I lost my job. The matter is politicised. I could go that root. There is media out there I could go that root. Since I'm a published Author there is no ways that I should be writing a book about this occasion

Most of you reading this book are going through staff at work. Like a vulnerable and insecure wife who keep on coming back to a very abusive husband. The reason is that many of you worked many years in the company and have accumulated a lot of debt and have all sorts of commitments onto you salary cheque. It becomes difficult to even open your mouth because certainly when you confront issues you might be the next victim. Your financial commitments are your strongholds. You'll drive a nice car, live in a big house, kids go to great schools and when this is the case loosing your job is no option. Especially when you live like most South Africans with accounts and bonds. Don't even think about being radical at work, you will be overthrown.

I) SEEK TO BE SELF SUFFICIENT

From the very beginning, I knew that I should not fully rely on anybody as those few zeroes in people's bank accounts can make a difference in their lives. I did not fully rely on my Union and neither political organisations. I had a pen and a paper that I knew would liberate me. It is very easy for union members to tell you that I would not make it into the meeting and there you are - thrown into the lion's mouth. Remember also that politicians are looking out for themselves in many cases and anything is possible. I have seen radical people hectically tackling issues out there of a noble cause but as soon as they are in positions of power to influence and improve the conditions of people who put them in those chairs they take another direction. I'm not saying that we should not trust that they can help us but you must back yourself. Let me repeat this statement, back yourself because at most cases you may need this backup as an individual to tackle issues with the little strength that you may have. The justice system cannot also be fully trusted because as you may look at the socio-economic spectrum of our country - the better of you is, the better chance you have of getting away with the justice system. This is a similar scenario with our health system. Equally so, you must seek to be self-sufficient financially and otherwise. One politician at some stage, whilst addressing the youth said that *we must stop dreaming of finishing school and go out there to work for a white man.* Particularly Europeans. Precisely because you will be institutionalised and therefore fail to realise your potential to liberate Africa and its people. As much as this statements may sound odd, or perhaps inconsiderate enough. People who are educated, especially blacks are the ones whom are at heart for Africa and are able to participate in the struggle of black people and the liberation of our brothers and sisters who have no knowledge and access to resources and understanding of Africa's riches and its independence from the colonial system.

Stay   Alert

I hear Politicians so many times talking about the majority and the minority issue in our country. White people constitute eight percent of our population. Their rate of birth is far below the majority in the country. Their average population is ageing and soon they will be constituting half of that the percentage they constitute currently. The fact of the matter is that if your majority race are bounded and their minds ruled by the minority principles infused in them, then you have your minority being the majority. Take a sample of the population in your community for instance. You'd have majority being black especially in the African context. In some communities, you may find even none whites. In your sample ask how many people are liberated from white supremacy. Please don't take this one likely. If you think that you can't function without the white's intervention then you are **institutionalised**. A lot of people are naïve about this word. A wise man once said that the danger of not knowing is that when you don't know that you don't know. It is better to know that you don't know, for then you may do something about it. I'm not talking here about getting a mere help from white fellows. I personally received one from whites. And I'm grateful for that to be honest. But I did not consciously think that without whites I cannot function. Even without their help, I was determined to do it on my own. How many are enslaved by white monopoly capital in your sample? How many like our fellow Somalians are making it on their own and generating revenue within their society? Perhaps a few. How many in your sample dress, talk, walk, practice consciously with an effort to imitate western civilisation. A black woman does not view herself or even perceived pretty if she is not wearing fake hair for instance. Yes it may look good on you and receive all sorts of compliments but in your subconscious mind - institutionalised racism is embedded. I have been there, done that in my institutionalised days. It may sound silly to you. But we see this kind of behaviours on our daily basis. So most of the time when you look at your results you will discover that over ninety percent of your sample population, their mind is set the way a colonialist designed it to be. I heard of something interesting that Americans have a set into their curriculum they teach. I stand to be corrected if I got this one twisted. They teach about how to be an American, How to embrace the colours of your country, How to embrace the national flag and etc. they are planting something into the subconscious minds of their people. That's why when you meet Americans they believe they are. We often think of them as arrogant. And that's not a wrong thing to do. It is the good value system embedded into their mind for survival purposes. My husband is training my children daily telling them how beautiful, intelligent, wise, pretty in their skin they are. That is rooting powerful words into their subconscious mind which will later rule their way of life and how they perceive themselves in a complex society. The colonialist did exactly that. Maybe I should ask you this question. If I may ask, What is it that is rooted in your mind? One other dilemma we have in our country is that any race other than white is regarded as black. Even Chinese falls within this category. There is nothing wrong with this. Well the purpose is for the BEE story we all know. It's a pity because many of such groups do not view themselves as black. It is only mentioned when getting jobs or a tender in particular to gain favouritism. Particularly coloured people in our country. They view themselves no where closer to being black. I speak about this because it's the race I came from. I can say much because I know and understand it better than any other race I know. Coloured people regards themselves as closer to being white. At least the majority of them believes so. And that is a problem when it comes to fighting white supremacy. This sickness is then going no were. Without realising it they are being used because they don't belong to the black but rather somewhere in between. I established myself long ago that I'm a Khoisan and that's what I am. A lot of coloured people wants to be associated with western civilization. I believe that has to do with the difference between poverty and richness. The history tells us about how the Khoi nation used to survive in the bushes and mountains. I guess people likes to be associated with anything the society regards as being the best. But that is the model designed by the colonialist. Apartheid did a lot of damage really, particularly the group act of Verwoerd. People from the non-white race find it difficult to work together in combating the supremacist. I'm not saying that we should team up and massacre the white community, well the way Zimbabwe did. But if we are one in our ideology and have a common understanding of how we would like to shape this land of our ancestors, we will surely achieve this. This matter has to be politicised. I hear a lot of people saying that they are not interested in politics. Believe me, I used to sing the same song for a little while. Let alone the involvement in which we leave in. Politics is everywhere. I don't know about animals but as far as there is human existence, there is politics. In fact, it is good to some extent. Well, at least to drive the economic growth. I have witnessed politics in the workplace, family squabbles, general politics, and unbelievably Church politics. Yes, I said church. People can murder each other even in the place of worship. Look at many religiously rooted countries that kill each other and terrorises many innocent lives. These people in most cases are very spiritual, but the politics within themselves overshadow the good religious practices they preach. So don't be naive. One way or the other you are involved in politics of some form. I just hope that you are not driven by the politics of your stomach because to be frank with you my friend, you are as good as a dead person.

Many employees make this mistake. They will team up with their fellow colleagues for a particular member. Many times for their boss. I witnessed this many times and once the person they team against is gone then they turn onto each other. When I arrived at Eikendal. I had a colleague whom was sick. She had a breakdown prior to my arrival because of the depression she had. The one side of her arm was on and off. She confessed to me saying that she had a hell of a time with the manager. She did not want to put a grievance because she wanted to get her money for twenty years of service. I thought to myself, do you have to wait twenty years going through trauma hoping to get the money that you won't even enjoy? Later when I was working there, when I had a case against the very same manager she was teaming up with. The very same person put her through trauma and she's teaming up with. How stupid can you really be? For real? This is a sickness that most of you have in your environment. Stop teaming up with others for wrong reasons. I had a senior friend working in Ravensmead library. When they approached her to team up against me she said to them, she's got a conscience. She wants to look at me in the eyes and greet me without guilt. These were her seniors. She did not compromise her principles because of her tummy. You may think about what opportunities she may have missed. Perhaps she was going get a better position or given more privileges but did not compromise her principles. Those are the compatriots we need in our society. Perhaps you are as well like that. At least I will be hoping. But if not then please you have to change. Otherwise, this monster called racism is not going anywhere in this country.

6

Women rights day Letter:

Thank you the MC,

The chairperson of **the party** Western Cape

The leaders of **the Party** Western Cape

Leaders of communities

Fellow Fighters and compatriots.

I have been tasked to talk about being Black conscious. Let me first clarify that saying black includes; Africans, Coloureds, Indians and Chinese as indicated in the constitution of this country. Black consciousness is a topic that our former struggle hero Steve Biko championed in his lifetime. It is indeed a subject close to my heart. And if you read my book that I have written (My first book) you'll understand why it is close to my heart.

I was made conscious of my blackness through the struggle of liberating myself and the writings of Steve Biko. Being black conscious is being aware of your identity and that should not be compromised. If, as black women, we lack reading and writing skills, we will be allowing the continuation of discrimination by the minority. Therefore, literacy plays a fundamental role in the life of a black woman. We need to involve ourselves in revolutionary movements and structures that liberate us and bring back the land which was stolen particularly to our Khoisan nation. This organisation, **the party** is our vehicle for our economic emancipation. Our fellow fighters, myself included are victimised continuously and discriminated while the perpetrator is enjoying the fruits of the land which was hard long fought for by compatriots who died in the process. When we speak about racism and white supremacy we are then perceived as extortions.

Our fellow comrades and colleagues out there are made to believe that certain things are and can be achieved by those who oppress them. White monopoly capital is a system made similar to the apartheid regime in order to manipulate our people not to see potential in themselves and to utilise their very own recourses for the betterment of their own communities. In fact, in most cases, the two work parallel to each other. We must be comfortable and proud in our blackness (Coloureds, Africans, Indians, and Chinese) and stand united so that the enemy cannot defeat us. We must stop accusing each other but rather to advise one another - in a way moving forward.

7

TAKE NOTE:

I volunteered my service to the City Of Capetown for over two years without a salary. When you decide to volunteer for the city of Cape Town there is no stipend, and there are no policies that protect you when you are black like me. Quite Frankly, there was a white lady at Bellville library who was volunteering but she was getting a stipend. Be careful, even if you are a volunteer from the city of Cape Town, make sure that you read the policies of the city of Cape Town and you abide by the rules. When you are a black person, you can never regard yourself as equal with a European at Bellville Library. You will suffer severe depression, go for counselling sessions and your medical aid allowance will even get depleted. Just remember to fight your own battles because there is no one who will fight them for you. During the time of grievance level 1 against my line manager. The district manager of District 5 and the director of the library services came out to show support to the line manager. All Chief librarians urged all staff managers to write negative reports about me and only two of those refused to write and the rest wrote such fallacies. This was done as to build the case against me. This is just to intimidate you and make you feel less. This was the highlight of my life. Most people who wrote negative things about me are as I write this book suffering in silence. They are Always complaining but don't have the backbone to confront this issue. The day I get a transfer in 2016 is the day they all will be victimised. Those who only have grade 12 will say Lendy I only have matric I cannot take on our line manager. I showily will reply back "you are permanently employed, you have a union that is your lawyer you have a big mouth but not a backbone." If you think xenophobia, it is a worse welcome to Bellville Library. Where your own brothers and sisters are bad mouthing you and writing dreadful and deleterious letters about you just so that you can get a disciplinary hearing and lose your job. Still, I do regard them as my brothers and my sisters. Again, this is how the successful apartheid regime have made our black people, designed them to be cruel against one another, and not only to murder each other but also to make sure that our sisters don't have jobs to feed their children.

Run away from conversations where staff members want to discuss only work politics with you. Especially if they have worked for more than five years' experiencing the same pain year after year. Run away, I call them plastic politicians. They can never stand up for the truth, they do not have the backbone to wear their SAMWU Red T-Shirt at work but rather wear it when they go to sleep where no ones sees it. These plastic politicians at your workplace will team up against you for the wrong reasons. Do not talk to them, just greet them back and remember, one day is one day, they will cry ten times worse than you and then no one will take them seriously because those negative letters that they were writing about you will haunt them to their grave. They will never be at peace at work or content even at home. You, on the other hand, will continue to make progress in life. You Have to build a strong relationship with your family, husband and children and those words they have written about you will come to live in them and within their children and they will be cursing themselves unconsciously.

I would like to give tips here because over two year's period I encountered and went through channels and systems of grievance procedures. It is up to you to take this advice but I was groomed by experts and people who had experienced the city in this regard. Do not rush to the CCMA. Follow internal procedures. Even though it will be hard and will not be in your favour but it is necessary. Or worse do not go to the bargaining council, take my advice. I know what I'm talking about. Do not ask the union for advice when you are at work in front of your colleagues - believe me, they are cameras. Someone is even hired spy on you and is busy recording every conversation you have. The very dear friend that will swap shifts with you, the very friend that will give you a lift home, borrow you R1000, will go and add spices to the story. They will inform the line manager that you have just asked a question about your job description and it was not even about your job description. And believe me, you did not even ask the union for that, you were just calling to find out if SAMWU members, for instance, are getting free t-shirts and if not how much does those cost. Then the Line manager will have a meeting with the management and then it's party time for you. Make sure that whenever you uses the telephone of the city of Cape Town you are alone, there is no friend meaning no SABC fake reporters. That's what happened to me.

I was called to the office for not greeting and smiling to white staff members who have the same job description as myself. That was simply because these people did not care anyhow of my existence. I was called in for sitting at the desk of an assistant librarian. I did not know that if you are a full-time white assistant librarian the city of Cape Town gives you a chair and a computer to sit on and you must not share it with other races specifically black people. If you are me, you are reprimanded and called to a meeting and forced to use the telephone in the workroom where you have no privacy or if you want to use the computer to check something on the ESS work programme to make sure that you check how much leave you have or you can upload your sick certificate. Just remember, when the city of Cape town line managers/senior librarians becomes aware that you have read and the policies of the city, especially the one that states the Employment Equity Policy for the city of Cape town and the one on one harassment - It becomes a problem. You become a threat to them. Do not make friends at work. At least I wouldn't advise simply because it's not a safe place, it's a dark dangerous territory. Focus on your development at work. I had to clean DVDs from the 2nd of September 2013 until the present. That's called slavery. It's called mental slavery and how can I be content with that? On 21 November 2014, I attended the Customer Relation Training at Millpark Johannesburg. For two days I had such a marvellous time a break away from the harsh political situation at work. I have learned that there is no batho principles at work nor open door policies. There is no transparency, information gets edited into a staff newsletter and we were told that the reason for that it's because some of the information are very sensitive. At Bellville, we did not get the same minutes as other libraries. It's either they are edited or omitted. Especially when it comes to the issues around rights. That's a bunch of lies from the LIASA Chairperson in the Western Cape. She does not want the staff to be informed and to develop, especially black people. Everybody knew about this but was hard to confront the matter. White supremacy is not going anywhere anytime soon in this province. We need a radical political transformation to mobilise black people.

If you are having the same job description as myself or earn below R7000 rand per month then join the South African Union for Municipal Workers also known as SAMWU. Never act out of emotions. If you experience any problem, don't just pick up the phone and call unions. Go to them. Even though they are useless in many cases you perhaps need a union for advice. It was useless in my case where I had to represent myself at CCMA. I have explained that in the letters chapter. Make sure that you speak to a Shop Steward, get the name, email and contact of that person and explain carefully the nature of the events with dates. If a patron laid a written complaint about you or even verbal, make sure that you have read it - it's your right to read what the next person has written about you. How are you going to defend yourself if you have not read what bad has been written about you? In my case, Europeans always make sure that they ask patrons to write a complaint about me and even to tell the patron that the line manager despises me. It is in their nature. I have witnessed one instance where a patron complained to a senior staff about a service, instead of solving the problem right then, she told the customer to please write a complaint. If you do witness such cruelty in your workplace, act as if you do not see anything, but make a mental note. Else you are the next victim. Never attend any counselling hearing by yourself, always make sure that you go to the battlefield with your union. Be a person of integrity and not adopt the dysfunctional behaviour of your line manager.

As much as we don't like it, be prepared and always ready to send an email to your line manager for whatever problem you encounter because that will be valuable at CCMA. Send your side of the story, remember, there is always two sides of the story. Not everyone is as strong to take on Europeans. Remember, when you do decide to take on your Line manager or any senior worker you will be victimised. Never talk to your friends about your grievances at work. I did not have a single friend at Bellville Library. Most of them were so called unpaid journalists who pretend to give you advice but in the meantime to get information out of you so that they can inform the line manager about your next step so that they can remain in good books.

Grievance Levels and advice

"Plastic politicians are those who love to sing revolutionary songs but a deadly afraid of white supremacy and controlled by the politics of the stomach, they mobilise the community to get votes but will never go to the CCMA and tackle racism "

I have emailed SAMWU several times asking for assistance on how to handle my situation at work. SAMWU suggested that I must put in a grievance. My union gave me the advice to put in a grievance but not willing to assist me on how to put it in a grievance form, meaning that I have to download the grievance procedure form from the website of the city of Cape Town or explained to me that once I have put in a grievance, I will forever be victimized at work. I had no choice. I had a choice that I can suffer and be slaughtered by demons (white power structure) in the city of Cape Town or speak the truth. I serve a living God. James 1 Consider it pure joy when you face trials because you know that the testing of your faith develops perseverance. I had no choice but to put in a grievance because the torture at work became unbearable. My line manager and her management made sure that they made my workplace an unpleasant working environment. I had no fear for the minorities. I developed hate towards them for always belittling me not just in their offices but at times in front of other staff members in meetings. when I wanted to raise an important issue I was cut off completely because of time or there is a lot more serious issues that management needed to discuss. I asked God for wisdom on how to tackle this injustice or bullying caused by apartheid agencies. I also had to keep in mind that my line manager made it very clear to me that she will never get punished by the government which is leading in Cape Town. At the time I was not sure what she meant but I made my request and made my supplication known to God. Memorise the ones that speak to you like Psalm 31 and Psalm 40. Psalm 40-22 He sits enthroned above the circle of the earth, and its people are like grasshoppers. This means no one is above God. The city can control CCMA in Cape Town but the city cannot control Jesus Christ. The city is a grasshopper in God's eyes, meaning a very tiny thing. There is no one above God no matter how painful the situation may seem, just persevere even if the policy has preferential treatment, it is for blacks but it does not mean anything to white people. I kept praying to God to give me wisdom on how to dismantle the system that ideologically is a mirror image of Verwoerd National Party Policy today known as Democratic Alliance.

I) INCONSISTENCY IS HER NAME – BULLYING ME WAS PART OF THE PLAN

Everyone feared my line manager at work. Some staff members even referred to themselves as slaves. This means that whenever we enter the door of Bellville Library, we would smile no matter how painful it may seem, just smile and think about the money that the city pays into your bank account every month on the 27th. I said over and over again that I am not a slave and I told other blacks that I will not be controlled by white capital and suffer in silence. God gave me this job not to be a slave. If money would be short in the till I would automatically be blamed for that, meaning I had to pay the money back even though I knew that, this was just a tactic to make sure that I get tired and resign. If others break the policy they would get an email saying that they must repeat the same mistake again. I get an email from the line manager, the Labour Relation Officer who is a German get called in to give me a counselling session and the very same thing I get counseled for I also get a disciplinary hearing for. God kept me going as I was about to give in, God gave me another scripture to hold on. I was hungry for His word and I know the battle that I am fighting at work is not against human governments but demonic forces that want us to continue to fear white supremacy and to make us believe that white is the head and we are the tail, meaning that we are less important and that our lives do not matter at all. I was surprised that Lokiwe Mtazi who have been employed in the city for 10 years as an executive director have never seen a problem with Bellville Library's white power structure after 22 years of democracy. Instead, she continued allowing them to tyrannise me during grievance level 3 and she did not even give me an opportunity to finish listening to my grievance level 3. Keep in my mind that at my grievance level 3, there were three SAMWU shop stewards. SAMWU is just created in Cape Town to create and make you believe that it is there. In actual fact is false hope. Here is the letter I have written for this grievance level one.

Cosatu (SAMWU) known to represents the ANC

SAMWU in the Western Cape gets all their funding from the City of Cape Town from Fax machines, chairs meaning all their offices and office equipment. Samwu members need to get that printed in their heads meaning joining Samwu as your union you on your own. Imatu (union) is even worse when you a black person. The only difference between IMATU and SAMWU is SAMWU members strike to get an increased meaning stay out of work and not get paid for that day makes sacrifices a IMATU members do not strike but still get an increase and even offer loans if you want to renovate your house, SAMWU do not have the capital for that they do not even have capital to issue T-Shirts for their members. IMATU gives T-Shirts and free cups. The day your find yourself in a real situation attaching an issue like racism you will be on your own. You need to stop joining SAMWU in strikes and singing. It does not help, it gives you false hope. It's either you do or die. Do not share everything with your union. Unions can be bribed just like commissioners at CCMA can be bribed. CCMA and the city are the same they promote white supremacy. For example, I have Subpoena Ninnie Steyn she was directly involved in my disciplinary hearing. There are similarities between CCMA and the City of Cape Town. For example, have issued me the Subpoena form in date 2016 but because Ninnnie Steyn is white on the day of the hearing the labour relation Officer Matt Stopka (German) said Ninnie will not come today she will come tomorrow to represent the city. How did that happen I don't know. I was the one that summoned her not the city. CCMA just like the city has preferential treatment. CCMA promotes the white power structure, for example in January 2016 during my Arbitration Ms Lokiwe Mtwasi said there was still issues pending during my grievance level 3 meaning she did not finish my grievance level 3 and ruled in the favour of Christelle (white). According to CCMA that is okay if a white person does not follow procedure/or attend a grievance level 3, it's okay if the city still rules in her favour there is nothing discriminatory about that. It's purely normal at CCMA. So if you do take any case against the state to CCMA just keep in your mind CCMA have preferential treatment. The commissioner asks the German where is his witness Cheryl Heymann on the 23rd October 2015 he respond Commissioner it is her 60 birthday today. Meaning because it's a white person birthday she was not able to avail herself. if you had an opportunity to cross-examine the witness like I did with the executive director just no one thing you will ask the question and the commissioner will answer for the executive. Like for example when I ask Lokiwe Mtazi about the date, why did she lie about the 29th April 2015? Why did she lie in her outcome of grievance level 3 in 2015 saying I was given charges on the 29th April 2015 and ruled that the city must continue with the charges when she knew that I was given the charges on the 20th April 2015. The commissioner answered for the ED what is so significant about the date. I had to explain that on that very same day of the 20th April 2015 at 9am I have escalated the grievance to level 3 on the very same day my white line manager issue me with four fabricated charges to silence me for speaking out against racism. Keep your shotguns to yourself. Refrain from making a noise in the streets in Cape Town and take matters to the court of law and you will see whether SAMWU can do the job or not. You will see whether SAMWU fears the union or not.

My shop steward forced me to sign the grievance form of level one. But I only received the minutes five months after the grievance took place.

However, the grievance made my line manager attitude became from bad to worse against me. She would refuse for me to attend certain skill courses offered by the city of Cape Town. When I question her about her behaviour she will say do you remember you have taken me to grievance level one and no one in the city have ever dare to challenge me. You are from lower levels and are not aware what you up against. She keeps on saying this is the political environment. Shame on her she was trying very hard to intimidate me instead she made me more and more suspicious. My colleagues at work told me very clearly that they can no longer have a conversation with me they would like it when I work with them to rather remain silent they do not want to victimised because one of them said her husband is not working the one said her boyfriend is only a local truck driver. I realised then these people are highly controlled by white capital the politics of the stomach. The truth does not matter at all but money that buys status is far more important than anything else in that matter.

My line manager decided to have a counselling session with me and the labour relation officer as if it was a serious offence that I have committed. Keep in mind the Afrikaner Brotherhood (AB) who were active during apartheid was also acting during this period having secrets meetings on how they're going to silence me for speaking out against racism. I have highlighted earlier in the book the things I was counselled for.

I waited six months for the outcome of grievance level one. Just remember the majority of Samwu shop stewards do not have a diploma in labour relations and therefore did not even bother to ask for the grievance level one outcome. My samwu representative had only a certificate of attendance and not competence there is a huge difference. He had so much fear in his eyes for the city. It was unbelievable but he loved singing and making noise in the streets with samwu members. I always say it's good to sing and jump and sing revolutionary songs but the real deal is put SAMWU in a real situation and see how it goes away from the journalist. I was supposed to receive the outcome in 10 working days, not six months.

The situation have gotten worse that I had to put in a grievance level 2

I have sent the chief librarian this email (see C.4 in the letters chapter) not just about the racism from patrons but also the ongoing Victimisation from another white staff member Louise Brink. She never dealt with this matter. Instead, she protected the white people at Bellville Library and gave me a premeditated counselling session form without following procedures.

Clearly, this is the evidence of Institutionalised racism whereby black people are being victimised and the system of inequality based on race. It's very clear white skin privileges is being promoted at Bellville Library. My line manager practised institutionalised racism against me a black woman deliberately and limit my rights as an employee. Let me not forget she won an award for 2014-2015 Best manager of the year in the City of Cape Town R20 000 for Bellville Library and R2000 from library staff.The meeting of grievance level 2 took place on the 9th April 2015 at 11h30 with Matt Stopka(German) the labour relation officer, Tania Alcock Smith (Khoisan chairperson), Denise Cleophas IMATU, SAMWU

Grievance Level 1 and Grievance Level 2 I was assistant by shop steward that had no backbone. He's got a loud mouth but make a noise like a puppy. Who voted for him to be shop steward is a story for another day. Then again you can nominate yourself if no one has vote of confidence in you. Grievance Level one took place at my workplace how intimidating but I kept persevering. Grievance level 2 was not chaired by the director but a Khoisan descendant who loves to be called coloured. The name coloured give some coloured people hope of being close to whiteness. Meanwhile, the director made all the decisions on the outcome of this level 2. This means her race is just but a white person has the final say, conscious versus Unconscious Discrimination.

Grievance level 2 I requested the content of the recording the Khoisan descendant refuse. She said there is no need for me to listen to the recording she will listen to it and decide. She also said there is no racism in the city. Perhaps there is something wrong with me. Swearing is a serious offence in the city of Cape town if it's done by black person swearing at a white person the white person will open up a civil case against you and sue your eye and ears. You may ask SAMWU it happened to one of our SAMWU members. Whereby a Khoisan have taken a white line manager to the grievance and then when the white person found it he/she immediately open a civil case against the SAMWU member. When SAMWU raise the complaint to the city and said this is pure intimidation the city says it's a civil matter there is nothing they can do about. Just a reminder when you register consider carefully if you vote for who because voting does not matter if you live in Cape Town. You can have all the proof/evidence at CCMA but if you have a case against unfair discrimination minorities CCMA will still rule in their favour. If a white person swears at the black person it's seen as okay the white person gets counselling and the black person who reported this matter gets to be further victimised and traumatised. Furthermore, this Khoisan said there is no racism at Bellville library I must get my eyes checked out. And told me there is something wrong with me. This clearly states to me that it's normal for white patrons to makes derogatory remarks about blacks and we must not feel offended.

The grievance level 2 took place on the 9 April 2015 on the very same day the Rhodes Statue was removed from UCT. That was history for me.

On this day the Mrs Ninnie Steyn the director who is heartless and cruel cannot fight her on battles have appointed a fearful Khoisan who works in HR as the chairperson. This chairperson praised and worshipped the Europeans that works with the city of Cape Town. How can you destroy your own people? Protecting white capital. The politics of the stomach. Protecting white supremacy even if it means preventing the truth from coming out by being honest and have integrity. I received the outcome of grievance level 2 on the 17 April 2015. The city of Cape Town clearly states that they gave me 5 working days whether I am satisfied or not. But here comes the funny part in the process of grievance level 2. I received a charge sheet from my very same line manager I have taken to grievance level 2. Pure intimidation. But I refused to be intimidated by her. She's not Jesus and will never be. The city have no shame thinking black means no brain, but in reality, black means bold. On the 20th of April, after I have accelated the grievance to level 3 the city HR department send me an email that ,"If required, I would then submit the completed grievance form with all the supporting documentation to level 3." I believe this woman assume that I am on cheap drugs because she refuses to listen to me during the meeting at grievance level 2. What makes her believe I must trust her I had lost all my faith in the system and will escalate until justice is served. God does not put His name to shame.

"Receiving an award for protecting the policy of Verwoerd's monopoly "

On the 20th April at 9am I have escalated my grievance to level 3 on the very same day I have received premeditated charges for the following:

1.   Insubordination for emailing a complaint or grievance to my employer on the 14 February 2015 (keep in my mind that I already received counseling for this specific charge)

2.   Negligence in that you failed the Declaration of Interest documentation required of municipal employees despite repeated request from your line manager to do so on or about the 6th February 2015. (keep in mind that my line manager is a chairperson of Liasa but has never declared to the city that she is doing private work to the city. She said Liasa is the professional body of libraries. This is extremely funny when I cross examine her in February 2016 I ask her if Liasa is part of the city she said no then I ask her if the city is part of Liasa she confirm no. I would like the readers to decide based on her answers if Liasa is indeed the professional body and what does that mean. What was even funnier when I ask her did the city ask you specifically to declare Liasa and that she is a chairperson she said no. Then I ask her did you specially ask me to declare my book she said no.

3.   Dishonesty in that you did not declare to your employer that you are published author and motivational speaker despite repeated request from your line manager to do so. (keep in mind, my line manager lied she had never sent me an email to ask me to declare that I am a motivational speaker or a published author. I was always open about the work that I do

outside the city in my own time. I have sent all the staff in the city emails (October 2014) that my book is out in 2014 in March 2015 I was live on SABC 2 talking about my book. There were several newspaper articles published about my book so there was clearly no dishonesty but I was open and honest about my book from day one.

4. This charge is called Alternative Charge 3 performing private work in that you have published a boonkie in the community on or about 4th September 2015. (Any blind person that can read clearly can see charge number 2, 3 and 4 is the same thing just using different words clearly fabricated.

The joke is my white line manager even confess at CCMA on record in February 2016 that she had never asked me to declare my book in any email or ask me specifically to declare my book or even ask me to specifically to declare that I'm a motivational speaker. My question is if she did not ask me how can she issue me charges for it. how can she issue disciplinary charges on the 20th April 2015? This clearly shows that this white line manager mandate is to oppress me for speaking out against the white power structure at Bellville Library. This is clearly her main objective was to keep the verwoerd's ideological legacy alive. Based on her ability to silence me, she received an award. Receiving an award for protecting the policy of the white monopoly. I don't care you may call it an award for whatever you call it but its what it is.

Grievance Level 3.

Five serious issues that was not dealt with, I was not happy with the outcome of grievance level 2, therefore, it was again within my right to accelerate the grievance to grievance level 3 including the following issues that the Khoisan refuse to attend to because of the politics of the stomach

1.   Recording of the 6th March. Done by Mrs Lubbe. This recording listened to the absents of myself and my union representative and the contents of it was concluded

2.   Transformation why after 22 years after democracy is Bellville Library Management still white.

3.   Intimidation-given notice of disciplinary hearing while we are busy with the grievance

4.   The unethical way of managing staff. Badmouth issue-not l listened to

5.   The issue of premeditated counselling form gave me counselling but not dealing with the swearing

It was helping getting the city manager to give her date. The city manager used all sorts of a delaying tactic to make sure this matter is not heard at all. SAMWU told me to have patients that the city have a lot of grievance of level 3 since 2014 waiting to be heard. Well, that was true. They, in fact, had over 100 grievances the city never dealt with and the majority of them were racism related. Those people have also had much more serious racism issues and their argument was what makes my case so important that I must get a date now. Really plastic politicians. I decided to email the city manager myself and told them I will put in a dispute with the city for not giving me a date. Finally, I receive the date for the 30 June 2015.

The DA/City Did not invite Christelle to this grievance but I had a grievance against her. Cheryl Heyman whom I do not have a grievance against came for the grievance, she was invited by the director for what I don't know.

If shop steward fear white supremacy ran away.

29 June 2015-30 June 2915

As a paid up SAMWU member I wanted whoever was going to represent me no need to be well articulated in English but radical and have a historical consciousness of the struggle of our people. Samwu must avoid losing grievances because as a result the working class particularly lower levels like myself loose trust in the trade unions. On my grievance Level, 1 and grievance level 2 the shop steward that represented me failed to prepare for counselling and hearings and performed poor as the results of lack of such preparations. On top of that, he had no idea how libraries operate or what is the job description of assistant librarian. On the day of grievance level 2 I remember him asking me What. This created an awake inside of me. On grievance level 3 another female assistant librarian from Delft South library represented me but couldn't defend me on the day of the 30th June 2015. It was obvious she feared the city of Cape Town. SAMWU needs shop stewards who will stand for and by the people against all odds. The ANC failed the black people in the Western Cape. Bellville Library needs a serious transition as I'm writing. The only thing is that even if you go there no and ask the staff of the things I'm talking about in this book, well they wont say much. Because that's how a capitalist institutionalised them. Will take you Job if you expose us. After 21 years of democracy, how can SAMWU allow Bellville Library to uphold and maintain the power structure of apartheid? Being an Alumni of UCT gave me the confidence to be an effective vehicle for radical change and to destroy the high levels of bureaucracy the city upholds for radical change.

The Assistant Librarian from Delft South all of sudden was assisting me with my grievance level 3 case. Bear in mind lady has been employed as An Assistant librarian for 20 years and told me herself that she is almost finished with her degree in library science and needs a promotional post from the city of Cape Town since she received the bursary from them to further her studies. I knew my case was in danger. I kept as if i am unaware that she's a spy (meaning a sell-out). She also lived in the dark side of Belhar where gangsters' were increasing and that became very clear she is poor and needed a promotion fast. Furthermore, she told me your case is strong but you must remember the city of Cape Town is much stronger and can destroy you. How can she say something so funny showing no remorse? I ask myself what is this woman doing is she working for SAMWU or is she representing the city. She keeps on asking me for more email I said I had none because I cannot afford to share with all my information all my shotguns. This woman is high bacteria infectious by the politics of the stomach fearing the white supremacy. She was so negative in the meeting I had with her. She wanted to forward all my emails to her and I only select which one because I knew I cannot trust her. She just wanted to know what is my grievance and what do I want from the grievance.

On the 30th June 2015

I received a call from the Delft South lady saying "Lendy the grievance on Level 3 is cancelled. I told her it's fine I'm still going. She then called me to ask if I can go to my bank and get my bank statements. I told her I am not going there I have enough proof. Her main goal was to mislead me. But by the Grace of God, I made it at the Cape Town civic centre an hour early.

Christelle Lubbe the one I had a grievance against is so powerful and decided not to attend Grievance Level 3. This clearly Indicates to me how powerful White people in the Western Cape are, so much Untouchable.White people remain in power controlling the entire Western Cape black people will team up with whites against black just for a promotional post or for fear of being victimising.

Archie Hearne from SAMWU decided to take over. Arlene was supposed to defend me because that's why I am paying SAMWU but because of the politics of the stomach (meaning wanting a promotional post from the City) she did not want to be in Lokiwe Mtwasi bad books and decided to just clarify what I was saying but not defending me at all. On the other hand, Mr Archie Hearne was defending and saying racism Lokiwe racism Lokiwe why don't you investigate Bellville Library.

Ms Lokiwe Mtazi undermined me throughout my grievance and I liked that when people look at my salary I get paid by the city of Cape Town automatically I get categorised in a box meaning empty vessel. When I spoke about transformation she said transformation takes 100 years. How can you even say that when you are supposed to sort out this issues. Then I like surprising people. She kept on echoing, people from the lower wage. The grievance was not finished. She spoke the majority of the time giving a ridiculous example of her friends wanting to join SAMWU. That's where the majority of the time was spent. She closed the meeting saying that the time was over and cannot give me another date as the matter was not finished.

In the City, there are three grievances grievance level one which is the district manager, the grievance level two which is the director and then there is a final and most important grievance which is grievance level 3 the City Manager. This is the three internal procedures one needs to follow if you would like to put in a grievance. Only after you received the outcome of grievance level 3 if you think it's being unfair labour practice you have every right depending on the nature of the case either submit it to in Bellville at Bargaining Council only if it is unfair labour practice but if it's about unfair discrimination you must submit at CCMA in Cape Town. Do not wait for assistance from SAMWU you must be on point, be careful do not give SAMWU too much information because your union gets funding from the city and therefore will tell everything you told him/her to the city. Keep your shotguns for yourself. SAMWU is inconsistent they decide which cases they would like to handle to score points in the city. Easy cases with hardly any evidence they will come and defend but serious cases like racism with evidence of recording and emails on black and white they will not come out to defend because of fear. Always remember when you do a grievance always make sure you have a smart cell phone. Delete all unnecessary photos and video clips of that cell phone. Clean your cellphone. Delete all unimportant pictures from your cell phone to increase your storage space on your cell phone so that you can record every single word. Always have two pens one will defiantly get dry and have a book including a highlighter to highlight important notes that you think it's essential. I'm saying all these things because most were the mistakes that I made at some stages. Remember you do not know how long your grievances will take place. Do not underestimate your line manager. The city will always favour them meaning internal procedures will never favour you. Keep in mind always mentally the day you put in a grievance level one on that very same day the white people are secretly planning your disciplinary charges. You must be at all times conscious at work. Do not discuss your grievances with your colleagues they are hunting for promotional positions and will be used to get direct information from them some will even use the word of God to get details from you and pass it on to your line manager when you not around and then he or she will get a promotional post because of your pain and suffering at work. During grievance procedure, if it's your time to talk immediately quote from the policy of the city and say your line manager is in contrast with the policy be clear. Treat your grievance level one just as a CCMA case. SAMWU do not prepare for grievance level one. I had to ask God for wisdom and prepare for my grievance level one because they take your suffering at work very lightly. Remember it's not SAMWU that is suffering you are just little paid up member to them nothing more. Even though without you SAMWU will not exist. Do not be a move by the presence of your line manager and district manager who is all white do not attend grievance level one without your representative (SAMWU/UNION). Be careful and listen how he argues if he is not doing something right correct him there and then if its racism its racism not inconsistency. Always make sure you provide proof/evidence and do not wait for longer than 10 days for the outcome of any grievance. Always remember while you waiting for the outcome of grievance city is busy preparing your disciplinary hearing or planning your exit. The majority of the shop stewards comes from the poor economic background or "wanna" be politicians looking after their own interest it is easy to bribe them. So be careful. Unions never prep with me I had to prep with the help from Holy God. God was my only hope during grievance level one and two.

Keep in mind once you put in a grievance the city will start looking for dirt in your life something to destroy you. Make sure you not found guilty of any criminal cases because they will use that against you. Before you write the grievance write down everything that had happened to you. To keep your side clean you must always send an email as proof that has communicated with your line manager and if she is not responding to your email resend it. Double check for the correct name and spelling. Keep notes of everything. Write it all down in detail. Do not sign anything the grievance form at all. It does not matter if your line manager is black or white make sure you have sent an email to cover yourself. You must receive the outcome of the grievance within 10 working days. On the 11 days if still did not receive the grievance minutes you must email your district manager and ask for the outcome. If you are not happy with the outcome you can take the grievance to grievance level 2 and include new matters if she has been victimising you or causing conflict at work. Make sure you have proof of victimisation at all times. For example, you applied after the grievance for a bursary to study a degree in library science and she refused that is pure victimisation.

The majority of SAMWU representative are not really wise and will tell you to sign because he does not study labour law he/she just received a certificate of attendance. So don't bother to trust their judgment. Atleast I can advice that.i have had quite an experience with them. Whenever I was at their offices I have encountered a lot of people, old men and women with huge family responsibility fired and SAMWU saying there is nothing they can do. I know what I'm talking about. Many have cried in my face begging for the union to help them. An old man once asked me to defend him, he thought I was a shop steward. That's because I was having a hectic argument with SAMWU about what I wanted from my case. I was radical about my case and they thought I was receiving a third cheque from some political parties. Can you believe it? The matters of the workers are not viewed as the matters that needs union's attention but rather matters of politics. If it's then so what are we paying the

unions for? Well, that's a book on its own for another time. But what I'm worried about is that this is a Trent. A lot of people are suffering out there in their working environment but unions fail them.to me, there is one thing that most unions like SAMWU are good at, Singing revolutionary songs.

8

LETTERS

(A)

My CCMA Closing statement

THE CCMA CAPE TOWN WESTERN CAPE

CASE WECT 12181-15

SAMWU OBO LENDY THOBEJANE (APPLICANT) AND THE CITY OF CAPE TOWN (RESPONDENT)

CLOSING ARGUMENTS.

1. Introduction

It is stated in Chapter two, section 9 of the South African Constitution that:

9. (1) everyone is equal before the law and has the right to equal protection and benefit of the law

(2) Equality includes the full and equal enjoyment of all rights and freedoms. To promote the achievement of equality, legislative and other measure designed to protect or advance persons or categories of persons, disadvantaged by unfair discrimination may be taken

(3) the state may not unfairly discriminate directly or indirectly against anyone on one or more grounds, including race, gender, sex, pregnancy, marital status, ethnic or social origin, colour, sexual orientation, age, disability, religion, conscience, belief, culture, language and birth.

(4) No person may unfairly discriminate directly or indirectly against anyone on one or more grounds in terms of subsection (3)

(5) Discrimination on one or more of the grounds listed in subsection (3) is unfair unless it is established that the discrimination is fair.

According to the City of Cape Town Labour Relation Officer Matt Stopka, one cannot rule on a grievance if it's not finished this was said on record at CCMA. This implies that the city is governed by rules and policies like any other organisations. This means that the city is therefore required to apply fair treatment across all the employees when implementing these rules

2. The Arbitration

2.1. Myself(applicant) referred alleged unfair discrimination dispute relating to Bellville library and the city of Cape Town after exhausting all the internal procedures (grievance level 1,2 and 3) of the city and conciliation(first Bargaining Council 13 August 2015 then CCMA) to the CCMA for Arbitration on the 03 September 2015.

2.2. The Arbitration was scheduled for 02 October 2015 and was postponed by SAMWU without my knowledge. It was eventually commenced on 23 October 2015. I (applicant) had to represent

myself because SAMWU did not come for the arbitration. This was the result of the SAMWU representatives not coming to the arbitration as they feared the city for most still receive a salary from the city(respondent) itself.

2.3. I presented my own evidence to substantiate the discrimination I have experienced at my workplace. I have subpoenaed the following witnesses to give testimony in this regard. Ms Jessica Mc Dillon, Ms Isabel Young, Mr Matt Stopka and Ms Ninnie Steyn. It should be noted that Ms Ninnie Steyn was supposed to be my witness but found at CCMA on the day 18 January 2016 that she will be the witness for the respondent and that she is not available on the day and will be available on 19 January 2016.

2.4. It should also be noted that I applied to subpoena Mr Archie Hearne SAMWU shop steward and Ms Patricia De Lille Mayor of the city of Cape Town as I believed they have information that could help in my case but the Subpoenaed was denied by CCMA without any explanation.

3. Transformation issue

The commissioner indicated clearly that the topic cannot be explored as she cannot rule about transformation in the city or

Bellville management structure.

4. Preliminary issues

This was my first time ever being in an arbitration representing my very own case. It should be noted that in this regard I was bound to make mistakes in terms of procedures and rules of conduct, terminology use and how evidence should be presented. Moreover, having to represent myself without any assistance as opposed to my respondent who is professional in the field and experienced and had an assistant was a huge task. Facing and cross-examining witnesses myself was an emotional task. English is not my first language and was a struggled in constructing sentences when asking questions.

When we begin the Arbitration on the 23rd October 2015 Commissioner have asked me not to switch on my recording and do a conciliation. In that meeting, Commissioner has told me that the organisation (respondent) only have R350 000 and do not have R10 million to offer. I have refused to settle for that amount. The commissioner has advised me to take it to labour court I told her I would like to argue it out in arbitration and if justice is not served then I would like to take this matter to the labour court.

5. Evidence presented

I will be referring to witnesses themselves and bundle copies in dealing with certain topics I believe to proof/disproof the allegations of discriminations based on race and/or conscience. In this regard what I believed to write and/ wrong about how the city have dealt with my grievances and matters I complained about.

6. Declaration of interest

The city requires every staff member to complete a declaration of interest form irrespective if private work is done on a voluntary basis or not and for financial benefit or not.

Christelle did not declare that she is a chairperson of Liasa. Cheryl Heymann, Ninnie Steyn and Matt Stopka defended the matter. Claiming that Liasa is a professional body. I argue that Liasa is an independent organisation and has absolutely nothing to do with the city and members join voluntarily at their own interest. On the 11th February 2016 Christelle Lubbe who is the chairperson of Liasa confirm on the record that Liasa got nothing to do with the city and the city have nothing to do with Liasa and that you can be a librarian and retire without joining Liasa. I further argue that professions like pharmacists, medical doctors, nursing cannot practise without registering with HPCSA (Health Professional Council of South Africa). In fact, you need to register while you are still studying. That's how serious it shows to belong to this body. However, it's not a case with liasa and librarians. In this regard, Liasa is therefore like any organisation found in communities and can join at your own interest. I was given charges for motivating children in poor township schools and poor communities by Christelle on the 20th April 2015 (See Bundle A p 112) and when I raised this issue with the city I was not listened to. Therefore I was discriminated based on race and conscience.

7. *Harassment/ intimidation*

Twice in the process, I was counteracted or attempted to be silenced when I complained to the line manager Christelle. First when I reported to her on the 6th March 2015 that Franzi Danz (white assistant librarian) was swearing at me she did not listen to my case and resolved it but instead, she gave me on the 6th March 2015 a counselling form (See Bundle A p 39). It is convenient to say it was the right time to issue such a form, I believe I should have been listened to first and resolve the matter of Franzi at the time I complained instead of giving me a counselling form.

Secondly when I escalated my grievance to level 3 in the morning at around 8:59 am (See Bundle A Page 73) to the city manager Christel again gave me the charges of a disciplinary hearing. In both scenarios, it is clear that Christel's intentions was to silence me each time I lay complain.

8. Transfer to Eikendal library

As I mentioned I did not agree with the minutes of level 2. Mr Stopka was present in the grievance when I mentioned clearly that I did not wish to be placed in district 5. I referred the matter to level 3 because I was not happy about how the grievance was conducted. While the processes of grievance level 3 was undergoing the District Manager Cheryl interfered with this processes and placed me in her district 5 when I made clear that I cannot be in district 5.

9. Email of Cheryl Heymann

The email that Cheryl Heymann wrote that I have played in bold a minor role and unsupported evidence (See Bundle C p28.2.1). I find it offensive and discriminatory for the city (despondent) knew about this matter very well in the 2002 case. Matt Stopka said on the 25th November 2015 here at CCMA that the content of the letter was wrong as I did not play a minor role in that case. I argue that it's absolutely not fair not to talk about this letter as it is linked to the 2002 case that has been ruled out by the commissioner. But the content of the letter written in 2015 referred to the matters of 2002. Therefore in this context, I'm speaking on the matter of the letter that was written in 2015 the email Cheryl wrote when I was in the grievance processes. I asked the Commissioner to look at the content of the letter within this confined date of my grievance processes. I found this email written by Cheryl Heymann to be discriminating against me based on conscience.

10. Recording of the 6th March 2015

Tania Alcock Smith at grievance level 2 concluded on the recording. My argument is how you can conclude on the recording without me having a copy or content of the recording in written form, while I was the one grieving against my line manager. I requested to Ms Tania at level 2 and Lokiwe Mtwazi at level 3 to listen to the recording and have the written content of the recording but both did not want myself and my representative SAMWU to listen to it. But they were able to both rule on contents of the recording. This indicates to you very well that city shows preferential treatment to my line manager more than my case. Furthermore the executive director at level 3 but still rule in Christelle Lubbe's favour on the matter.

Therefore I was unfairly discriminated based on race and conscience.

11. Mayor Patricia De Lille intervention

I have alerted the mayor Patricia De Lille about my grievances with SAMWU (See Bundle D p11). Matt Confirmed on the 23rd November 2015 there was a mayoral intervention meaning that the mayor did know about this matter. In the minutes of the intervention, it was stated that the mayor made recommendations about my grieved issues but I did not get any feedback from the mayor about my grievances. The respondent confirmed the document I presented at CCMA about a mayoral intervention that the mayor knew about my case. On the 11th February 2016, Christelle witnessed confirmed that she was never communicated in any form or through channels by the mayor about the approval of my sick leave and the issues I grieved about. Mayor is the head of the city and I expected her to pay attention to the matter since I have exhausted all the levels and she was the only hopeful communication channel I could rely on. The mayor gives me false hope (See Bundle D p1). It is therefore clear that the mayor did not find the issues that I was grieving about important and perhaps the agreement she had with SAMWU about my case was just a hopeless promise. The respondent did not disproof this matter because he knew that it is true that Mayor did not care. In this regard, I was discriminated on conscience.

12. Witnesses

12.1. Jessica Mc Dillon: Assistant Librarian she ran a successful programme at Bellville Library even though she did not have a Four Year degree in Library Service. Jessica indicated that she is a friend of Christelle and Bellville Library certainly she would've known the fact that you cannot run a programme without a degree and have been working for the city for many years. In her own words, she clearly stated that you do not need a degree in library science to run a programme at Bellville Library. She ran successful drama programme at the library on her own and if she assisted a librarian she would've clearly stated this. She confirmed on record she only assisted the launch of the teenage section and safety programme She further indicated she will not challenge her boss as she does not want to lose her job. Jessica worked for the city for many years thus she knew and understood the system in the city of Cape Town very well. And this shows clearly if you challenge your boss certainly you will be victimised and might lose your job in the process. Which is what Christelle told me before. Therefore since she was in good terms with Christelle she was given opportunities to explore her talents and gifts. Therefore in this regard, I was unfairly discriminated based on conscience.

12.2. **Isabel Young**: Children Librarian. Confirmed that she does not have a four year degree in library services instead she has a B-TECH in Police Service. She was employed as a children librarian and run programmes without a four year degree in library and information science. It is now when I mentioned this matter at CCMA that she decided to resign end of January 2016 from the city. It should be noted that I did not grieve the position she held but she was tasked to run programs and work with children without required degree but I was however denied to run programs. There in this regard, I was unfairly discriminated based on race and conscience

12.3. **_Venive Robo:_** _Senior Librarian. Confirmed that she did not declare prior 23 November 2015 that she is a Liasa member, owning properties which she is renting, that she is pastor's wife running a church. She indicated she was not told before to declare. She only declared now in January 2016 Because Cheryl Heymann told her to do so (See Bundle D p36). If this declaration policy was fairly implemented she would have declared a long time for she has been working for the city for the past 10 years and that she is a senior librarian. This rule was only forced to me and therefore I consider this unfairly discriminated based on race and conscience_

12.4. **_Christel Lubbe:_**

Christel confirmed on the 11th February 2016 that she never came to me and ask me to specifically declare for either book or that I do motivation in my spare time. She was not asked to specifically declare that she is a chairperson of Liasa in the Western Cape. No one came to me or written to me specifically that I should declare my book or that I do motivational talks but was charged. Ms Lubbe was the one serving me with both charges for counselling and disciplinary hearing. If she believed that I was wrong and did not adhere to the policy of the city concerning declaration why did she plan to counsel first (See Bundle A p107) with other issues of misconduct and leave out the *declaration issue for the disciplinary hearing? This page (See Bundle A p107) Indicates that both scenarios were planned at the same time by Mr Stopka, Christelle, Cheryl and Flippie. This is clear that she was fabricating this charges to work me out. Furthermore, she counselled me (See Bundle A p74a) on the insubordinate issue and then disciplined me on the same issue. This issue was withdrawn after I argued with Mr Stopka and given a proof that yes I was first counselled for. Only then Mr Stopka withdraws the issue. Christelle indicated in bold that I was dishonest (See Bundle A p74b) about that I published a book in the charges. However, she confirmed on the 11th February 2016 that I did inform her that I have published a book. She even confirms that she acknowledge the book in the staff newsletter for everyone to read that I have published my first novel. The commissioner should consider this charges and how they were framed because it is clear that the motive behind was to silence me. Therefore I was unfairly discriminated based on race and conscience.*

12.5. **Lokiwe Mtwazi**: *Executive Director. She confirmed at CCMA in front of the Commissioner that grievance level 3 was not finished there was still matters pending at the end of our* meeting. She did not give another date to finished the matters even though I had issues that I needed to be resolved and I was not fully listened to

A)   Lokiwe ruled that I must stay at Eikendal Library and should not be moved even though I told her I cannot work under Cheryl Heymann under District 5. This indicates that she refused to listen to hear by cry and it doesn't matter I can continue on being harass by the district manager. She further ruled that I did not get an injury on duty when I ask for the city to cover my medical cost.

B)   Lokiwe lied about the date in her ruling. She indicated that I was given the charges of the disciplinary hearing on the 29th April 2015. I have given her evidence that I have been issued disciplinary charges on the 20th April 2015 the day I escalated the grievance to grievance level 3. (See Bundle A p112) I have grieved about this matter with Lokiwe and in her ruling indicates clearly she did not wants to listen to me but was authorising as indicated that the disciplinary hearing should continue and take place.

C)   Lokiwe the executive director confirmed that she did not declare for attending liasa conference. In her words, she clearly indicated at CCMA that there was no need for her to declare that she was attending a conference. This evidence points out clearly even the executive director does not see a use to adhere to this declaration policy but however, the city expect me to declare and if I don't I, therefore, get disciplined.

D)   It should further be noted that in her decision she relied on the minutes/ outcome of level 2 grievance which I did not agree with and comments from Cheryl Heyman. In this regard, it was imperative that Christel is present in which she was not present in the hearing so that both parties can give their versions of the story. It was for this reason that the grievance was not finished. points A, B and C above I, therefore, consider myself being unfairly discriminated based on race and conscience

12.6.   Matt Stopka. Labour Relation Officer. On the 23 October 2015

Matt stressed many times at CCMA that you need a four year degree to run programmes in the library and information science. Furthermore, he stressed that we the employees of the *city need to adhere to the declaration of interest policy. The city failed to apply its policy to all the employees. His witnesses that he brought here at CCMA*

(12.3, 12.4 and 12.5 above) failed to adhere to this policy. Therefore the credibility of him should be questioned as this policy were not advocated with fairness. Matt was involved in this case from counselling, grievance level 2, disciplinary hearing and he knows the details of my case and still stresses the policies and present the witnesses he knows that failed to adhere. Therefore it is obvious that I was discriminated simply because I have challenged the system.

13. Conflict at work

(See Bundle D p35)It has been said that I did not get along with staff and line manager at Eikendal Library. However being at Eikendal was not my choice in the first place. I have grieved this matter with the executive director. She believed Eikendal is the right place for me and ruled against my wish to remain there. The City cannot expect me to be happy there when I gave the Executive Director my reasons for not being there. I suffered harassment (See Bundle D p31.2)at Eikendal. Veniwe Robo handed me charges of declaration whereas she did not declare herself. How am I expected to get along with somebody giving

me charges whereas the very same person is bragging about she did not declare. She continuously harasses me with my rooster (See Bundle D p33 and p34) and that she wrote wrongly with a pencil. Furthermore, she discusses with staff members and Cheryl Heymann my medical condition without firstly discussing with me and provide wrong information in the process. She did not correct my time sheet on my ESS properly at work. In this regard, the city cannot ask me to be at peace with my line manager.

14. Conclusion

Considering the matters above I, therefore, ask the commissioner of CCMA that as you rule on this matter please consider the matters that I have raised above. The respondent failed to disproof (see point 11 above).The respondent witnesses above failed to adhere to declaration policy to the city like myself and the city did not find any fault with it. I did not fill the declaration of interest at the time like them but was charged. This clearly indicates that since I have been complaining about racism, harassment, victimisation, and intimidation in the workplace I *was discriminated based on race and/ conscience.*

(B)

July 16, 2014

Mrs Christel Lubbe (Chief Librarian at Bellville Library)

Carel van Aswegen Street

Bellville

7530

My name is Lendy Thobejane. From 2011 till 2013, I volunteered on a full-time basis at Ravensmead Library. In September 2013 I was successful being appointed as a Part Time Assistant Librarian at Bellville Library.

It saddens me to raise my concerns w.r.t transgressions against me. By ignoring these issues and the ongoing verbal assaults, I can no longer tolerate.

These events ultimately led to my current situation and I feel this is the opportune time to address them to avoid further unhappiness.

Section 9 (2) of the Constitution provides that

(a)Equity includes the full and equal enjoyment of all rights and freedom.

In September 2013 I asked Mrs Lubbe if I can participate in the Ama-boekies also known as the Reading Competition of the City of Cape Town. She gave me the go ahead and informed me that the Amaboekies is a competition for everyone. Anyone can participate. On the 29th November 2013, Mrs Lubbe emailed me and Cornita Phelps the Reading List of the Ama-boekies. I made reservations on my library card and immediately start reading during the December holidays. During the month of January 2014, I made quite a few notes of the characters, places and events. During this period Ms Elize de Jager told me she doesn't understand why I am reading the books for the Ama-boekies because Mrs Lubbe will never select me to represent Bellville Library.

I told Mrs Alta Oostenhysen (Senior Librarian) that I so exist about the Ama-boekies. Mrs Alta Oostenhysen told me, "Lendy, Christelle did not mention your name when the City of Cape Town (During the DMT Meeting) asked for the names who is going to participate in the Reading Competition for the City of Cape Town.

On the 21st February 2014, I read the Staff Newsletter and my name was not on the list to participate for the Amaboekies. On the 22nd February (Saturday) I was working with Mrs Lubbe on the same shift in the morning. I asked her Mrs Lubbe why my name is not mentioned for the City of Cape Town Reading Competition. Mrs Lubbe stated the reasons why my name was not taken for the City of Cape Town Reading Competition, "The City of Cape Town does not know me since the city of Cape Town is not familiar with my name I cannot participate and according to the District Manager, I have no behaviour skills. I replied back by saying that the City of Cape Town cannot discriminate me like that, The City of Cape Town must give everyone an equal opportunity to participate. She said well that is the City of Cape Town according to the City of Cape Town I'm just a newcomer and there is nothing more.

In March 2014 Mrs Lubbe called me and told me the City of Cape Town said I can participate. I was confused first the City said no and discriminated against me and now the City of Cap Town said yes. On the 19 March I emailed the District Manager Mrs Cheryl Hymann and cc Mrs Lubbe the truth why I am not going to participate in the reading competition in the email I stated:

"I am very grateful that you have given me the opportunity to participate in the Amaboekeis for 2014 but unfortunately I already have thrown all my notes away that I have made between December 2013 and February 2014 about the names, dates and places of the characters including cars and events that

were taking place on the books in February when I was told that those who are in charge of the amaboekies only preferred names that they are familiar with. And because they do not know my name I cannot participate. I fully understand so that's the reason I had to withdraw in the first place."

Confidentiality

6.2.1 Grievance about discrimination shall be investigated and handled in a manner that ensures that the identities of the persons involved are kept confidential as far as reasonably possible.

On the 27 March 2014 at 13:40 I had a counselling session with Mrs Lubbe, myself and a Representative of SAMWU Mr Sidney Flusk only.

Mrs Lubbe wanted me to attend this counselling session because I emailed Mrs Cheryl Heymann. According to Mrs Lubbe I had no right to email Mrs Cheryl Heymann if there is conflict in the management regarding the City of Cape Town Reading Competition. After the meeting, Mrs Lubbe went to Mrs Alta Oostenhysen office. Straight after that Mrs Alta Oostenhyisen called me in her office with an open door with Mrs Lubbe standing at the door listening to our conversation. Mrs Alta said that I have no right to mention her name during the counselling session and I do not understand that I am only a 5-hour worker and do not understand my job description. I replied back and told Mrs Alta it's clear that she had no right to confront and victimise me about the counselling session that took place earlier. She was not part of the meeting and Mrs Lubbe had no right to discuss my privacy with her as stated in the clause 6.2.1. I also told her I am not just a part time worker, I am a university graduate and that is very clear I was not employed at Bellville Library to develop but rather employed because of Affirmative Action.

In the constitution of the City of Cape Town, it clearly states

•The focus of the City is to develop current, internal employees.

On the 25th, 26th, 27th November 2013 and 2,3 December 2013 I was doing a short course on Children and Youth Literature at UWC. On the 12th December 2013, I wrote my feedback form and Mrs Lubbe called me into the office and forced me to rewrite my training form and resubmit another form. In this attachment, you will find my original one. She said that I must only write good things about Bellville Library and I told her that this feedback form was for my own personal development and I should not be told what I must write because I have to be honest about how I felt.

Experienced Racism from the patrons/Customers

30th December 2013 at Circulation Desk I was badly insulted by so called white patrons. Because of this insults, I made a mistake on the till. Torn the slip out of receipt book it out because the two incidents that just happened to me I threw it in the bin. Mrs Lubbe called me in January 2014 in her office and told me that If there is money being stolen from the till in future she will have me responsible for the theft. She told me I will walk out of this library with only a bag when she is finished with me.

According to the City of Cape Constitution

•Merit may not be determined in a manner that is arbitrary, nor is the length of experience the only criteria to the exclusion of all other criteria. Formal Qualifications, relevant experiences, prior learning and the capacity to acquire ability (potential) within a reasonable time should be taken into account.

On the 15th October 2013 I emailed Ms Ninnie Steyn regarding a structured Reading Programme that is running at Ravensmead

Library that I would like it to be taken further beyond just one library but across the Library Services in the City of Cape Town.

On the 3rd December 2013, Ms Ninnie Steyn replied back via email and said I must make contact with the District Manager as the potential first step.

On the 22nd January 2014, Ms Lubbe called me into her office and said that Ms Ninnie said that I must forward the email to her and she will forward it to Ms Cheryl Heymann (District Manager). On that specific day, she called me in and ask me what exactly is this reading programme about at Ravensmead Library I told her it includes poetry reading, play reading, professional storytelling and puppetry to bring stories and characters in the book to live. She said it's not what the public library needs but she will forward to Ms Heymann. With the same breath she said if Ms Heyman has not replied to her email regarding the proposal it means that is unsuccessful without giving me the opportunity to do a proper presentation.

It has been 5 months. I had no reply for Ms Cheryl Heymann. When I asked Ms Lubbe when can I present this reading programme proposal to Mrs Heymann. She told me there is no need. Mrs Cheryl Heymann said that I am only a 5-hour worker, and she has no business regarding the reading programme proposal. She also told me Mrs Heymann said I have no degree in Library Science to do a presentation for Mrs Heymann. I told Mrs

Lubbe but I have been running this reading programme for two years successfully, I am a graduate in theatre and performing arts and with these skills will benefit the reading programme and she told me a no means no. no one cares about the reading programme at Ravensmead Library it is a small library.

The Lendz Reading Programme are being discriminated by the City of Cape Town

Principles of the City of Cape Town

5.1 COCT wishes to create and maintain a working environment which is free of discrimination where all employees respect one another's integrity and dignity, privacy and their right to equity in the workplace.

I emailed the children librarian that I want to start a Theatre in Education drama club for the children in the library. Mrs Lubb said no I must stop emailing them proposals. I am just a Part Time worker. I do not know how to run any theatre programmes at the library and told me I have no experiences in running it.I am willing to elaborate on these and other issues at your earliest convenience and at a time suitable for all of us to find a mutual solution.

Sincerely,

Lendy Thobejane

(C)

Grievance Level 2

The grievance Level 2 was escalated on the 11 March 2015. The grievance meeting was scheduled by the city of Cape town on the 9th April 2015 at the LIS Head Office at 53 Berkley Road, Maitland in the Gordimer Boardroom.

A grievance against Ms Christelle Lubbe (Chief Librarian at Bellville Library)

After 20 years of Democracy, this is how black people are still suffering under the hands of those who were in charge during the apartheid regime. One would think working for the city of Cape Town is an opportunity but it's an opportunity to be Victimised, racially attacked and forever been discriminated. The history of apartheid repeats itself over and over at Bellville Library via Chief Librarian Christelle Lubbe. Who not only victimise me but creates conflict amongst staff members. I have been emailing my union about the victimisation that Christelle lubbe is doing to me.

1) 08 December 2014 03:42 PM I have emailed Christelle Lubbe about why is she badmouthing me by another staff member Xavier January. The email reads as follows:

Dear Christelle

On the 6th December 2014 @ 13h30 in the AV Room Xavier January complained that I bad mouthed him by Christelle. Christelle I humbly apologise for sending you this email but this confrontation created conflict amongst staff members. I told Xavier that not once did I ever bad mouth or report any staff member by Christelle in her office. If so can you please tell me when I came to Christelle's office to complain and what I have said because Xavier is very angry at me for complaining about him by Christelle. The reason why I email you because I tried to solve this matter with Xavier but Xavier refused to believe me, therefore, I refer this matter to you because this matter creates conflict at work.

Christelle refuses to call a meeting with myself and Xavier because she knows very well she is making sure that everyone at work despises working with me. She creates conflict for me with everyone. This matter was never dealt with.

2) Section 9 (2) of the Constitution provides that

(a) Equity includes the full and equal enjoyment of all

rights and freedom.

6.2.1 Grievance about discrimination shall be investigated and handled in a manner that ensures that the identities of the persons involved are kept confidential as far as reasonably possible.

On the 6/3/2015 I received my notice of counselling session with Mrs Lubbe, myself, Marrietjie Messenger and Francis Danz .

Franie Danz was the staff member who verbally attacked me by swearing at me on the 6/3/15 but yet I am the one that received a letter for counselling. This is very clear that if a white person swears at a black person its okay it's not taken seriously but I believe if this was apartheid the other way around I would have been killed. Francis Danz was not supposed to be part of the meeting when I was called it by Ms Bessinger to into Christelle's office for a Notice of Counselling Session.

On the 6/3/2015 Franzie Danz was swearing at me in the AV room just after I told her in at the circulation desk very nice that she must click on submit. Franzie was busy packing books nicely on the trolley and forget to do it. Franzie was so mad and shouted at me at the circulation desk ", Ï have been working here for the city of Cape town for more than 25 years", you thing. I ignored her. I continued with my work serving patrons. I then *went to the AV room to collect DVDs. Elize De Jager also white did not know that I am in the AV room and told Franzie in Afrikaans,""vat die ding aan man, vat die ding aan man" meaning take on this thing. This is very clear that these white people are out to attack me personally. Elize was so surprised when she turned around and saw me and immediately went straight to her desk. I did not say any word. Franzie then came in and told me, ""Ek sal nooit saam met die ding will work nie"" she said, she never wants to work with this thing. Referring to me as a thing. I told her ""ons is werk colleges en n span ons moet leer om saam met mekaar te werk meaning We are colleagues we must learn to work as a team. She replied,"Jy moet ophou kak praat".meaning stop talking shit. This white lady even confesses in front of chief librarian Christelle Lubbe and Senior Librarian Marriejie Bessenger that she did swear at me and that's nothing, she usually swears at her husband at home. Marrietjie one of the librarians was defending Fanzie that she did not swear at me and in this insidance, I realised that the white staff is teaming against me. Instead, Christelle recorded me on her cellphone and told me that Ms Cheryl Heyman said this is the only way forward to record me so that they can nail me. Mrs Lubbe did not deal with this matter instead she asked me if I was going to open a case and if so she will nail me with disciplinary hearing alleging that I was shouting at her. I begin to wonder if this is the city policies that the chief librarian must record staff meetings.*

Hence this is the reason I wanted this matter to be dealt with at the directors level. Because if Ms Cheryl Heyman can advise her to do this (recording) somehow Lubbe and her crew are teaming up against me. Are these what the city promotes? Because I wonder if black people have a place in this level of governance.

3)   In the previous grievance that I had with Mrs Lubbe, it was agreed that I will be moved and given opportunities and training to work in other departments. Is it only what a black assistant librarians does only to work at the circulation desk for 4 hours straight with only 15 minutes tea break and then one hour of admin work while most of the white people who are having the same job description as myself are able to work in other departments and not at the circulation desk. I strongly believe that I have been robbed to grow and to develop within the library services. Believe me, this has begun to decrease my enthusiasm and interest to work in such an environment and hence I have been demanding transfer and it looks like the matter is not going anywhere.

*4)   **Experienced Racism from the patrons/Customers***

The ongoing insults of patrons: I have sent Christelle an email about the following:

As Ms Christelle Lubbe requested an email from me regarding what happened on the 14th February 2015. Here is the email:

It was very busy at the counter only two people working. Myself and Roja Moodley.

A white female was asking me why are we so slow at the counter. He told me I must speed up. I told her very nice and slowly, "mam we are only two people at the counter and we are trying to assist the patrons as fast as possible ". She kept on saying but you must speed up. This lady was very impatient but I advised her if she has queries there is a librarian at the reader's advisor that can assist her.

Another white male complained to me about the long queue again. I explained to this man the same situation that we are only two people at the desk. This man went on and on by telling me that we know how busy the library is on a Saturday why do we only have two people at the desk. Again I asked this man to please go to reader's advisor there is a librarian who he can speak to. Or he can email our chief librarian. He refused.

A lady with her daughter came to me and ask if I can print something for them from smart case. Before I print I asked the daughter if she can come and have a look before I can print it for her. I then asked her again if she is happy. She agreed. I then press print. She paid for the two printings. After she received the printings she was not happy and demanded a refund because she said she only wanted a specific article. I told the lady and her daughter but I have asked you twice if you happy and if I can press print then you agreed. I advised her that I will give her extra time on smartcape and she asked me to assist her on smartcape regarding printing. I then referred her to reader's advisors because of the long queue. The reason why I referred her to the reader's advisors was because of the fact that we were only two assistant librarians on duty at the desk with a long queue.

Soon afterwards Louise Brink (children librarian) came to me very rudely while I'm on duty at the circulation desk and asked me where the lady's newspaper was. I couldn't answer her because I was busy with a patron. So I waited for tea time and try to explain to her what had happened at the desk. Louise Brink refuses to listen to me and told that I am forever making trouble at the desk and Christelle is aware of that and she will take this matter/complain to Christelle. How can Louise Brink make such a bad statement about me? She never works at the circulation desk or with me. She must stop victimising me.

Regards

Lendy Thobejane

(D)

SAMWU

Lendy Thobejane

Thu 2015-06-25 02:34 PM

Sent Item

To:

Archie.Hearne@samwu.org.za; Sidney Flusk; Patricia De Lille; Papikie@samwu.org.za;

'Mikel Khumalo' <mikel.khumalo@samwu.org.za>;

Cc: Goretti Francisco; Edmund Jacobs; Keith Lakay; Ninnie Steyn; andre.timotheus@gmail.com; umcedi@gmail.com;

Goretti it's you again. PAY BACK MY MONEY!!!

Firstly email my union Mr Archie Hearne or Sidney Flusk at SAMWU office not me regarding my salary. You (the city of Cape town) have already deducted money from me and told me I will not get it back again. Must I forward you my emails that you stated it in black and white? I will not allow the city of Cape town to put my family through hell again. It's 21 years of democracy and black people are still treated as slaves. PAY BACK MY MONEY. Black lives matter. It's because of the city of Cape town I was on sick leave (depression)in the first place. SAMWU must stop racism in the western cape.

I am well aware that Christelle Lubbe (City of Cape Town) have caused this it's called Promoting White Supremacy. The city of Cape town is clearly promoting the Legacy of apartheid by taking a big portion of my salary. Just because I have been taking them to grievance Level 3 for promoting white supremacy, Racism, Victimization and Discrimination.

DISMANTLE WHITE SUPREMACY IN THE WESTERN CAPE!

No emails. PAY BACK MY MONEY

Lendy

(E)

Lendy Thobejane

Tue 2015-06-30 06:15 PM To: Archie.Hearne@samwu.org.za; Patricia De Lille; Papikie@samwu.org.za; 'Mikel Khumalo' <mikel.khumalo@samwu.org.za>; Cc: Sidney Flusk; andre.timotheus@gmail.com; bdjoseph3008@gmail.com; umcedi@gmail.com;

Good evening Mikel Khumalo

WHY IS THE CITY OF CAPE TOWN PROTECTING BELLVILLE LIBRARY??????????????

WHY MUST A BLACK PERSON SUFFER!!!!

WHY WHEN I SAID THERE IS NO TRANSFORMATION AT BELLVILLE LIBRARY THE ENTIRE MANAGEMENT IS WHITE. MS LOKIWE REPLIED ITS 21 YEARS AFTER DEMOCRACY NOT A 100 YEARS.

I would like to salute Comrade Archie Hearne for fighting for me today without fear or intimidation in Cape Town Civic Centre in Lokiwe's office. amandla!!!!!!!!!!!!!!!!!

Christelle Lubbe the one I had the grievance against was not presented at all. My is the major promoting white supremacy.

Funny enough Mr Khumela, Christelle told me that I can never take her on. Bellville Library is the face of the city of Cape town in the Western Cape. I must Congratz the Major for again proving that the City of Cape Town promotes white supremacy.

But Ms Lokiwe the Executive Director refuse to listen to us. She said there is no racism at Bellville Library. We have never finished the Grievance Meeting on Level 3 because she HAD OTHER IMPORTANT MATTERS TO DISCUSSED.

Mrs Lokiwe refused the following:

1. She refuse to give us the recording that was done on the 6th March 2015 that was requested in the grievance

2. Admit that the City of Cape Town promotes White Supremacy.

how can Lokiwe gives us minutes of grievance level 3 if we didn't even finish the meeting? How is she going to put together the outcome??????????????????????????????????

3. Refuse to give me an opportunity to mention what I want out of the grievance.

3. 1 I told her I want the city of Cape town to pay my medical bills because of the city of Cape town I had exhausted all my funds and SAMWU MED refuses to pay for it.

3.2 I told Mrs Lokiwe I want Cheryl Heyman to withdraw from her previous statements for saying I have unsupported evidence and played a minor role in the Senior Librarian Molesting Innocent Children in the Library

3.2 I want Cheryl Heyman to write me a written apology for putting me through trauma and harassment.

3.3 I want the city of Cape town to give a written report on what happened to Mr Mays Case since I am the one that reported it in the first place in 2012

3.4 I want to be transferred from District 5 from eikendal library

3.5 I want Franzie Dans to be dealt with the way I was dealt with (equal treatment)

LONG LIVE THE SPIRIT OF JOE SLOVO, LONG LIVE THE SPIRIT OF TATA MADIBA, LONG LIVE THE SPIRIT OF HELEN SUZMAN, LONG LIVE THE SPIRIT OF STEVE BIKO

I WILL NOT STOP FIGHTING WHITE SUPREMACY IN THE WESTERN CAPE UNTIL BELLVILLE LIBRARY HAVE BEEN DEALT WITH.

I WANT TO BE HEARD!!!!!!!!

THE CITY OF CAPE TOWN MUST STOP FAVOURING WHITE PEOPLE. THE MAJOR AND HER TEAM MUST STOP THE LEGACY OF APARTHEID.

AMANDLA!!!

Lendy

Patiently fearlessly waiting for the outcomes of Grievance Level 3. Grievance Level 3 remain unresolved recorded on my cell phone on the 30 June 2015.

Lendy Thobejane

Mon 2015-07-06 12:02 PM

Sent Items

To: Faried Shariff; Achmat Ebrahim; Patricia De Lille; umcedi@gmail.com;bdjoseph3008@gmail.com;

Cc: Archie.Hearne@samwu.org.za; Sidney Flusk; Papikie@samwu.org.za; 'Mikel Khumalo' <mikel.khumalo@samwu.org.za>; Lendy.Swartbooi@gmail.com;

Sandra Shamrock;

Good Morning Mr Faried Shariff (The chairperson of my disciplinary hearing)

"At the heart of this kind of thinking is the realisation by blacks that the most potent weapon in the hands of the oppressor is the mind of the oppressed"

Steve Biko address on "White Racism and Black Consciousness", Cape Town, January 1971.

I need to bring to your attention on the 2nd July 2015 I received a date for the 15 July 2015 for my disciplinary hearing from Cheryl Heymann (Level1) via my temporary line manager at Eikendal Library Ms Veniwe Robo. Ms Veniwe Robo received it via email from Cheryl Heymann. With a witness present Ms Sandra Shamrock.

This happens after our Grievance Level 3 hearing with Ms Lokiwe Mtwazi the Executive Director. Ms Lokiwe have told Cheryl Heymann several times to stop victimising me. On the 30th June 2015 at the Cape Town Civic Centre in her office, Ms Lokiwe made it clear to SAMWU and myself that if Cheryl Heymann shows any form of attack she will deal with her personally. Cheryl Heymann (chief librarian at Bellville Library), Christelle Lubbe, Ninnie Steyn (Director of LIS), Charl September have already destroyed the reputation of the city of Cape town. Christelle Lubbe did not even attend the Grievance Level 3 hearing. Because she knows that she is guilty of promoting White Supremacy at Bellville Library and Keeping the Legacy Apartheid Alive alive.

We are still waiting for the outcome of grievance Level 3 from Ms Lokiwe Mtwazi. She does not even listen to her manager which is Ms Lokiwe Mtwazi. This is evidence that the city of Cape town is indeed promoting white supremacy.

Christelle Lubbe of Bellville Library told me,"No one ever in the city of Cape town have taken Bellville Library to a grievance of Level 1, we will make an example of you". The Charge Sheet of four charges is what she meant by making an example of me just because I reported Racism within the city of Cape town at Bellville Library. White people are so powerful in the Western Cape that they do not need to attend Grievance on Level 3.

I receive a disciplinary charge sheet for Being a Black Motivational Speaker for voluntary visiting townships and promote reading through reading programmes and storytelling but it is okay for a white person for swearing at a Black person at Bellville Library. SAMWU members are suffering in silence because if you report White Supremacy, Racism you will be targeted.

"A fearlessness evolved

Steve Biko

On the recording on the 6th March 2015 recorded by Christelle Lubbe on her cell phone.

If possible I would like to request a suitable date for this hearing to take place on the 31 July 2015 (Friday). Please keep in mind we are still waiting for the outcome of the grievance Level 3. Ms Chery Heymann must stop Promoting the Legacy of Apartheid. Stop interfering with grievance Level 3 she is on level 1.

Mr Faried Shariff, I hope to get a positive response from you. Both parties can agree on a suitable date. After the grievance Level 3 outcome

Regards,

Lendy

(F)

From: Lendy   Thobejane

Sent: 21   December   2015   12:02   PM

To: Ninnie Steyn; Patricia De Lille; Achmat Ebrahim; 'Mikel
Khumalo';   newfranktalk1@gmail.com
Cc: Papikie@samwu.org.za; Shamielah Jansen; Lokiwe Mtwazi;
yerushka@gmail.com;   Lindsay.maasdorp@gmail.com;   Ian
Gordon;   Desiree   Howard;   Nyanga   Library;
Gugulethu.library@capetown.gov.za; bdjoseph3008@gmail.com;
Phatiswa De Wet; Abigail Jafta; Elizabeth Dumane; Sunell Lotter;
Tirzah Arendse; Velna Konstabel; Roja Moodley; Claremont
Library;   Xavier   Januarie
Subject: Re: Communication: Verwoerd Legacy Continues

Attention: Ninnie Steyn

Verwoerd Legacy Continues

According to Verwoerd apartheid was just a matter of good
labour policy. Verwoerd ideology. In 2015 known as the ideology
of the City of Cape Town.

The aim of apartheid was to uphold the Afrikaner white
domination and the exploitation of black cheap labour

domination.

Protect the right of the white working class. Never have equal rights as the Europeans.

Most of my supremacists are German, we still have European instituting their own ideology in our land. And most of my oppressors are such and the city have bureaucratic tendencies.

For two years I worked as a slave for the City of Cape Town under the supervision of Ms Isabel Young a white woman at Ravensmead Library running theatre and poetry classes for the city without any payment even though I had the qualifications. According to the City of Cape Town policies if you want to be a librarian employed by the City of Cape Town you must have a four year degree. This white woman librarian was employed without a four year library science degree ever since she was employed as a librarian in a black library. This is evidence that the city practices the policies of Verwoerd whereby whites are highly favoured. Putting whites first. She only received her qualifications as a librarian in 2014. White Supremacy.

On the 20th April 2015, I became more vocal at work about white supremacy and accelerate grievance to grievance level 3. On the day of the grievance, the white woman who I had a grievance against never came instead her manager who is also a white came to speak on her behalf as if she's my line manager. Again Verwoerd policy is evident that whites and blacks do not have equal rights in the working environments. Verwoerd's policy is to protect the right of the white working class. The city still rules in her favour in the outcome of grievance level 3 even though the white woman never attends. Verwoerd policy.White Supremacy. Whites are highly favoured.

On the 20th April 2015 on this very same day because I became vocal I received four premeditated charges for not filling in a declaration of interest which is part of the policy of the city of Cape town. A white woman Christelle Lubbe who is the chief librarian in the city did not fill in the declaration form herself and admit it to the city and said she is a chairperson of liasa but not doing liasa work during council times. A black person received a written warning myself and the white woman who committed the same crimes remains untouchable. Blacks must obey the policies of Verwoerd which is today known as the DA Helen Zille political party that favours white people.

On the 30 June in 2015 City Of Cape Town said during grievance level 3 Christelle Lubbe is inconsistent and needs more training then Helen Zille awards her in September 2015 for best manager meaning awarding racism. Christelle received R20 000 for again keeping the legacy of honourable Sir Hendrik Verwoerd alive.

On the 30 June 2015 the ED Lokiwe Mtwazi who is employed by the DA when I asked her about Bellville Library whose management are completely white after 21 years of democracy and that we want transformation. the DA said it is not 100 years. Must we as blacks wait for 100 years for transformation. It takes time. Who are you fooling? HeH!!!!!!!!!!

On the 23 October 2015, the city asked me for my University of Cape Town qualifications. They asked me, "did you complete your studies in theatre and performing arts at UCT where is your proof". On the 23 November 2015 I provided the city of Cape town with my proof of academic transcripts surprise the white woman who is earning R18 000 every month who was never asked for academic transcripts from university yet as a black woman who gets paid R6000 was asked university qualifications. White Supremacy.

My line manager currently, Veniwe Robo and her librarian in charge Sesande Mtyi have been successfully harassing me at work controlled by a white monopoly. My very own black sister teamed up with whites and decided to be a witness for the DA for my case against the city which is about unfair discrimination-racism, and promoting white supremacy. This again for the politics of the stomach. On the 23 November 2015, I have given the city evidence of how Veniwe Robo have successfully victimised and harassed me at work. In December 2015 because my Veniwe Robo is a witness in a case against her own. The very same Veniwe Robo have been promoted by the DA to a Principle librarian not on merit on her continues vindictive behaviour towards her black sister. Veniwe Robo will start in February 2016 with a fat salary as a principal librarian at Claremont Library.

On the 18th December 2015, Ninnie Steyn came to eikendal Library in kraaifontein to promote and reinforce Verwoerds policies. She asked me to follow the policies and procedures of the DA. I refused to uphold the legacy of Verwoerd as a black person. If white people are not following the procedures why should a black person? Ninnie Steyn had the nerve to come and talk to me in person about my behaviour but when I was sexually harassed in 2012 and thrown out by the police officer like a dog for speaking out against Verwoerd's legacy. She was nowhere visible.

Bureaucracy is a district form of government, it does not represent democracy. It's a threat to individual freedom. To enhance the truth of political progress resist change. whites take pride in Verwoerds policies and will not change in the city of Cape town which is an establishment environment.

Go ahead Ninnie and institute whatever Verwoerd considered morally correct. But I remain fearless. I have followed channels that you claim to be communication which is useless to help black people in this regard for two years. "Racists want us to stop talking about racism, but they made zero effort to stop acting as such".

I have a case at CCMA going for Three Months. But your administration channels which you want me to report to are not stopping even for a day to harass me. Instead, they are rewarded for the legacy they are upholding. So you may institute a disciplinary hearing with your fellow oppressors and supremacist certainly no to me.

Why should I be treated like a slave in my own country? It is not a privilege to exists in this democracy and political landscape but it is my birth right to challenge the issues that my parents have suffered and continuing to mushroom in this dispensation.

I am not scared to loose money, career or whatever you do with people who are vocal about these tendencies. Either way, I win. Because I would have not on my consciousness compromised the ideological principles that Steve Biko was murdered for. Many characters have been shaped and compromised by the politics of the stomach, but I refrain from such act.

The Fearless Khoisan Descendant and daughter of Azania

(G)

From: *Ninnie*   *Steyn*
Sent: *18*   *December*   *2015*   *03:43*   *PM*
To: *Lendy*   *Thobejane*
Cc: Sunell Lotter; Lokiwe Mtwazi; Tania Alcock-Smith; Wesley

Terence *van* *Heerden*

Subject: Communication

Good afternoon Lendy

I refer to the attached e-mails and my conversation with you at Eikendal Library this afternoon.

I hereby confirm that I have given you a direct instruction to comply with the City's reporting lines, communication procedures and communication channels with immediate effect, failing which disciplinary action will be instituted against you.

Regards

Ninnie Steyn

Director: Library & Information Services

Ground Floor, 53 Berkley Rd, Maitland

Tel: +27 21 400 3782

Fax: +27 86 576 1398

Mobile: +27 82 656 2759

E-mail: ninnie.steyn@capetown.gov.za

Website: www.capetown.gov.za

(H)

Dear Honorable Mayor-From a Khoi-San descendant to another Khoi-San descendent

Inbox X

Lendy   **Thobejane** *8/11/15*
<Lendy.Thobejane@capetown.gov.za>

to Patricia, Achmat, Babalwa, Mikel, Gerhard, Archie.Hearne, Papikie, jerome.septemb., vvactor, yerusha, andre. Timotheus,

Desiree, Wilhelmina, Eleanore, Ian, me

An Open letter to our honourable Mayor Patricia De Lille

Good Morning Mayor Patricia De Lille

"Our kindness has been misused and our hospitality turned against us. Where whites were mere guests to us as their arrival in this country they have now pushed us out"

Steve Biko

Mrs Patrica, you are fully aware on the 20th April 2015 in the morning at 9 am I have accelerated grievance to level 3 to the city manager for Bellville Library that promoted white supremacy, victimisation and intimidation. On the same day after 1h20, I received four fabricated charges. According to Steve Biko, my charges is "deliberate creation of an artificial fabrication of the truth by power-hungry people whose motive is an authority". I consciously chose the word fabricated because the people who initiated this charges they themselves serve in various independent organisations while working for the city like myself. The matter is welcome to be investigated. I have been charged so I must close my mouth about the pressing issues the struggle of our people of the land. I had to attend this hearing for 6 hours defending why I did not declare my book to the city. It was this long in which I believe it was to test my mental capability.

It has come to my attention that I'm targeted yet there is majority of people in this municipality owning massive properties, some beach homes that they are renting, some owning farms, and others serving in various positions in various organisations and community structures yet not declared to the city. Therefore it goes without saying that I have been a target for talking about white supremacy.

I have exhausted all your administration levels in the city of Cape town and even had to attend a disciplinary hearing orchestrated by the city of Cape town on the 31 July 2015 (Bellville Civic HR Department) in the process. Yes, it is fair that politicians should not interfere with the administration of municipality. In this regard, it is, therefore, my plea to you madam that you clean your administration. For it will be ugly for the third form the come and do it for you. You publicly asked Mr Ramaphosa to give you proof of injustice brought to the people in the city as a result of racism. I trust that this issue of eradicating indirect racism and white supremacy is one among the top of your list, and therefore will be dealt with appropriately.

My conviction as a descendant of the people of the land is the liberation and emancipation of the cardinal pillars of the freedom charter and of our struggle in this democratic dispensation without fear and intimidation.

I would like to give you this gift for women's month August 2015 that you please clean your administration.

Rooting out apartheid tendencies in the mother city

Equal Treatment and Black Lives Matter

Lendy

(I)

From: Robin Moses

Sent: 11 August 2015 03:14 PM

To: Lendy Thobejane

Cc: Patricia De Lille; Taryn Hoosain

Subject: RE: Dear Honorable Mayor-From a Khoi-San descendent to another Khoi-San descendent

Dear Lendy Thobejane

Your email to the Executive Mayor, Patricia de Lille, is acknowledged, the content thereof noted.

Kindly note; your correspondence is receiving the necessary attention and please be advised, this office will revert to you within due course.

Kind regards

Robin Moses

Specialist Clerk: Office of the Executive Mayor

6th Floor I Podium Block, Civic Centre

12 Hertzog Boulevard, Cape Town

Tel: 021 400 2507

Fax: 021 400 1315

Robin.Moses@capetown.gov.za

(j)

On 17 Jul 2015 2:37 PM, "Lendy Thobejane" <Lendy.Thobejane@capetown.gov.za> wrote:

Dear Ms Lokiwe Mtwazi

On 17 Jul 2015 2:37 PM, "Lendy Thobejane" <Lendy.Thobejane@capetown.gov.za> wrote:

Can you please give me the outcome of my grievance Level 3. Its long overdue. Mrs Lokiwe Mtwazi why are you refusing to give me the outcome of grievance level 3. Mrs Lokiwe you are part of the child molestation conspiracy. You agreed with the white people that I must be removed from Ravensmead Library after I reported child molestation in 2012. You are part of the team that destroyed the lives of innocent black children. You are representing the DA. The DA is responsible for the child molestation that took place in 2012. It's the same DA that is refusing to give me the outcome of my grievance Level 3. It's the same DA that have put four fabricated charges against me for 1 for emailing counsellor Sonnenburg, 2 for publishing a book called Boonkie in the Community, 3 for not filling in a declaration form that I am a published author in the UK, 4 for doing private work being a motivation speaker for motivating black children to get out of poverty just because I reported white supremacy in the City of Cape Town. The DA (Lokiwe Mtwazi) made sure that white people do not need to attend grievances on Level 3 because they are powerful in the Western Cape. The DA is promoting white supremacy in the Western Cape. The DA is misleading the black communities in the Western Cape. The DA is the author of this ugly system called institutionalised racism. DA is continuing with their racist and oppressive system. Verwoerd's National Party today knows as the DA has no respect for black people. History will be written and recorded.

I have done it the Mandela way it's time to do it the Steve Biko way.

From: Lendy Thobejane

Sent: 15 July 2015 01:27 PM

To: Lokiwe Mtwazi; Patricia De Lille; Papikie@samwu.org.za; Achmat Ebrahim; 'Mikel Khumalo'

Cc: umcedi@gmail.com; andre.timotheus@gmail.com; bdjoseph3008@gmail.com; Babalwa Mothibi; Gerhard Ras

Subject: FW: Outcome of Grievance Level 3

Good day Ms Lokiwe Mtwazi (Executive Director)

Yesterday was the due date for the outcome of grievance Level 3. I have sent you and email yesterday and would like to ask you today can you please give the outcome of grievance level 3.

I have recorded this grievance of level 3 and you said we must give you 10 days. Today is the 11 day.

Kind Regards

Lendy Thobejane

(K)

On 17 Jul 2015 2:37 PM, "Lendy Thobejane" <Lendy.Thobejane@capetown.gov.za> wrote:

Dear Ms Lokiwe Mtwazi

On 17 Jul 2015 2:37 PM, "Lendy Thobejane" <Lendy.Thobejane@capetown.gov.za> wrote:

Can you please give me the outcome of my grievance Level 3. It's long overdue. Mrs Lokiwe Mtwazi why are you refusing to give me the outcome of grievance level 3. Mrs Lokiwe you are part of the child molestation conspiracy. You agreed with the white people that I must be removed from Ravensmead Library after I reported child molestation in 2012. You are part of the team that destroyed the lives of innocent black children. You are representing the DA. The DA is responsible for the child molestation that took place in 2012. It's the same DA that is refusing to give me the outcome of my grievance Level 3. It's the same DA that have put four fabricated charges against me for 1 for emailing counsellor Sonnenburg, 2 for publishing a book called Boonkie in the Community, 3 for not filling in a declaration form that I am a published author in the UK, 4 for doing private work being a motivation speaker for motivating black children to get out of poverty just because I reported white supremacy in the City of Cape Town. The DA (Lokiwe Mtwazi) made sure that white people do not need to attend grievances on Level 3 because they are powerful in the Western Cape. The DA is promoting white supremacy in the Western Cape. The DA is misleading the black communities in the Western Cape. The DA is the author of this ugly system called institutionalised racism. DA is continuing with their racist and oppressive system. Verwoerd's National Party today knows as the DA has no respect for black people. History will be written and recorded.

I have done it the Mandela way it's time to do it the Steve Biko way.

From: Lendy Thobejane

Sent: 15 July 2015 01:27 PM

To: Lokiwe Mtwazi; Patricia De Lille; Papikie@samwu.org.za; Achmat Ebrahim; 'Mikel Khumalo'

Cc: umcedi@gmail.com;   andre.timotheus@gmail.com; bdjoseph3008@gmail.com; Babalwa Mothibi; Gerhard Ras

Subject: FW: Outcome of Grievance Level 3

Good day Ms Lokiwe Mtwazi (Executive Director)

Yesterday was the due date for the outcome of grievance Level 3. I have sent you and email yesterday and would like to ask you today can you please give the outcome of grievance level 3.

I have recorded this grievance of level 3 and you said we must give you 10 days. Today is the 11 day.

Kind Regards

Lendy Thobejane

(L)

From: *Lendy* *Thobejane*
Sent: *12* *December* *2014* *01:53* *PM*
To: *Cheryl* *Heymann;* *Lendy.Swartbooi@gmail.com*
Cc: *Xolani* *Diniso*
Subject: Regarding Storytelling at Bellville Library (Highly Confidential)

Dear Ms Cheryl Heymann

According to our Grievance Procedure meeting that we had with Christelle (Chief Librarian) and Ms Heymann (District Manager) made it very to me that I am a Five Hour Worker meaning TCOE employee meaning I'm employed to work at the circulation desk and 1 hour of admin. You made it very clear to me that I must not do any storytelling inside the library or any other programmes because I need a four year degree in Library Science and on top of It. You made it very clear to me that the City of Cape Town does not pay five hour workers to do storytelling. Only when I have a four year degree that I can do storytelling and creative writing programmes at the Library. I fully understand that and respect your and Christelle's decision. The children librarian (Louise Brink) was against me and told me that I am not needed in the children section and she can do her own storytelling. She was even the one that told me I must go and study Library Science. And now she wants me to storytelling.

Ms Heymann you said that the Children Librarian must do her own storytelling because she get paid to it. Ms Louise Brink the children librarian at Bellville Library wants me to do storytelling for her holdiday programme on Monday the 15 December

2014 and I told her that Ms Heymann and Christelle made it very clear that I can assist with storytelling not do the actual storytelling. Ms Heymann can you please explain to the children librarian what is my job description regarding storytelling. She does not understand and this however creates conflict at the library.

If possible Ms Heymann I have never received the minutes from the meeting of the Grievance Procedure Meeting that we had at Bellville Library can you please forward it to me.

Kind Regards

Lendy

From: Louise   Brink
Sent: 12   December   2014   09:57   AM
To: Lendy   Thobejane
Cc: Christelle   Lubbe;   Alta   Oosthuizen
Subject: Stories tydens vakansieprogram.

Lendy

Ek vind jou verskoning waarom jy nou skielik nie wil lees nie onaanvaarbaar. Toe ek jou gedurende die week gevra het om te lees vir die vakansieprogram het jy geen melding gemaak *daarvan dat Cheryl jou tydens die 'grieviance procedure' belet het om stories te lees nie en wel ingestem om te lees. Dit is ook nie wat Christelle aan my oorgedra het nie. Jy het ook geen melding daarvan gemaak in Oktober toe jy wel stories vir die vakansieprogram gelees het nie. Jy het ook nie toe aangedring op 'n brief van Cheryl om te se dat jy mag lees nie. Ek gaan hierdie saak verder neem.*

Louise Brink

Librarian: Children's   Department   :Bellville   Library Library and Information Services

Carl   van   Aswegen   Street,   Bellville

Tel:	*021 444*		*7164*
Fax:	*021 948*		*9313*
Cell:	*074 129*		*7379*

E-mail address: <u>louise.brink@capetown.gov.za</u>

(M)

---------- *Forwarded* *message* ----------

From: Lendy Thobejane <Lendy.Thobejane@capetown.gov.za>

Date: Fri, Oct 2, 2015 at 10:52 AM

Subject: No postponement for the 23th October 2015

To: "Papikie@samwu.org.za" <Papikie@samwu.org.za>, Mikel Khumalo <mikel.khumalo@samwu.org.za>

Cc: "Archie.Hearne@samwu.org.za" <Archie.Hearne@samwu.org.za>, Kashief Soeker <MogammadKashief.Soeker@capetown.gov.za>, "Lendy.Swartbooi@gmail.com" <Lendy.Swartbooi@gmail.com>

Good day Mr Khumalo

As you are all well informed our new date for Arbitration at CCMA is on the 23th October 2015. I want no postponement. If Mr Khumalo or Kashief Soeker is not there to defend me again on the 23th October 2015 at CCMA for Arbitration I will have to go in to Arbitration alone and defend myself.

Lendy

Forwarded message ----------

From: Lendy Swartbooi <lendy.swartbooi@gmail.com>

Date: Wed, Aug 12, 2015 at 4:21 PM

Subject: Regarding tomorrow

To: Archie   Hearne   <archie.hearne@samwu.org.za>

Good day Archie

Are u coming tomorrow to represent me. If not ask Mr Khumalo to send someone else of SAMWU for tomorrow

(N)

Forwarded   message   ----------
From: Lendy Thobejane <Lendy.Thobejane@capetown.gov.za>
Date: Tue,   Aug   11,   2015   at   1:31   PM
Subject: Outcome of my Disciplinary Hearing is a Disaster: Stop Promoting   White   Supremacy
To: Patricia De Lille <Patricia.DeLille@capetown.gov.za>, "Papikie@samwu.org.za"   <Papikie@samwu.org.za>,   Mikel Khumalo   <mikel.khumalo@samwu.org.za>
Cc: "Archie.Hearne@samwu.org.za"
<Archie.Hearne@samwu.org.za>,   Keith   Lakay <Keith.Lakay@capetown.gov.za>,   "bdjoseph3008@gmail.com" <bdjoseph3008@gmail.com>,   "andre.timotheus@gmail.com" <andre.timotheus@gmail.com>,   "jerome.september@uct.ac.za" <jerome.september@uct.ac.za>,   "Lendy.Swartbooi@gmail.com" <Lendy.Swartbooi@gmail.com>,   "vvactor@aol.com"

<vvactor@aol.com>

Good day Again honourable Mayor Patricia De Lille

Why is the city of cape town ever going to stop promoting white supremacy.

I just received the outcome of my disciplinary Hearing. Its a disgrace. A white woman who put this four fabricated charges against me for doing private work and not filling in a declaration form did not respect the rules of the city of cape town herself. She herself never declared to the city that she is the chairperson of LIASA or doing private work for LIASA. Please feel free and investigate this matter.

(0)

---------- Forwarded message ----------
From: Lendy Thobejane <Lendy.Thobejane@capetown.gov.za>
Date: Mon, Aug 3, 2015 at 1:52 PM
Subject: FW: Declaration of interests form
To: Veniwe Robo <Veniwe.Robo@capetown.gov.za>, Sandra Shamrock <Sandra.Shamrock@capetown.gov.za>, Brenda Lufele <Brenda.Lufele@capetown.gov.za>, Dumisani Dayimani <Dumisani.Dayimani@capetown.gov.za>,
"Lendy.Swartbooi@gmail.com" <Lendy.Swartbooi@gmail.com>
Cc: Matt Stopka <Matt.Stopka@capetown.gov.za>,

"Archie.Hearne@samwu.org.za"

<Archie.Hearne@samwu.org.za>,   Faried   Shariff

<Faried.Shariff@capetown.gov.za>

Dear Ms Veniwe Robo (Line Manager of Eikendal Library)

All of us must fill this form in. Even if you are a LIASA member. I was made aware there is a policy on declaration of Interest on the 31 July 2015 during my disciplinary hearing. I thought that you can declare via email like I did in October 2014. Whereby I declared via email that I am a have published a book to the city of cape town. I was officially informed by Christelle Lubbe (chief librarian of Bellville Library) Charl September, Matt Stopka of Labour Relations and Faried Shariff on the 31 July 2015 at Bellville Civic that I must fill this Declaration of Interest Form in. Christelle Lubbe had not filled in the declaration form herself which is this form that is available on the intranet from the city of cape town policies. Even though she was fully aware of the policies and that there is a policy on the declaration of interest. Christelle had never declare on this form that she is a chairperson of LiASA Organisation. Please ladies and gentleman no emails you must fill in the form.I have heard than none of you had ever seen the declaration form or knew about the fact that even if you are not running a business but you are a member of a registered organisation other than the city of cape town you must declare. I have done my part by informing you. So that you do not end up like me being charge for not filling in a declaration form yet she (Christelle Lubbe Chief of Bellville Library) had not fill in the declaration of Interest Form herself. With my second book I'm aware that I must fill in a declaration of Interest form. The form is in this attach document. If you are not clear speak to our line manager. No emails. You must fill in this form and give it to our line manager.

Kind Regards

Lendy

From: Charl September

Sent: 02 August 2015 09:22 PM

To: Lendy Thobejane;

Subject: Declaration of interests form

Dear Lendy,

As promised, I've attached the Declaration of Interests form for you to complete and submit to your line manager.

Regards,

Charl September

Senior Professional Officer: Acquisitions

Collection Development Unit

(P)

She never filled in the declaration form to declare that she is chairperson for LiASA. She never filled in the declaration form that she is doing private work during city of cape town time for LIASA. As a matter of fact investigate now where she is now and going to be from the 13th August until 21 August during city of cape town working time. But because she is white its okay for her to abuse counsel times. Because she is white person she is allowed not to declare. This is cruel. I will not tolerate white supremacy in the western cape town.

Dearest Mayor Patricia De Lille can you please give me date when are you going to stop promoting white supremacy and how you are going help the city of cape town to stop promoting white supremacy.

I am a black woman and deserves the same respect as a white women. I want equal treatment.

All I am asking is for a date on when are you going to put a stop to the city of cape town for promoting white supremacy.

Today I filled in the Disclosure of Interest Form to declare that I will be volunteering at the IFLA conference. The form is in my line managers Office on her desk. I am black woman I must declare. A date please. Just a date when are you going to assist your management to Stop Promoting White Supremacy. How many evidence must I provide for you. Please indicate the numbers of many proof of evidence you need in order for the mayor to act radical on white supremacy.

Kind Regards Lendy

(R)

From: Lendy   Thobejane
Sent: 23   July   2015   12:37   PM
To: Veniwe   Robo;   Patricia   De   Lille;   Achmat   Ebrahim;

Archie.Hearne@samwu.org.za

Cc: Faried   Shariff;   Matt   Stopka

Subject: No Integrity

Dearest Veniwe (Senior Librarian of Eikendal Library)

You have called and forced me yesterday on the 22th July 2015 to sign and I refused infront of Sandra a staff member. Why do you lie and say on the form that you have sign it on the 15th July 2015. I have told you several times not to get involve. You only sign the form on the 22th July 2015 (yesterday) and made as if you sign it on the 15th July 2015. Its clear that you are part of this child molestation conspiracy. I will mention your name. You have no integrity. You are only doing this for promotional post.

(S)

----------   Forwarded   message   ----------
From: Lendy Thobejane <Lendy.Thobejane@capetown.gov.za>
Date: Thu,   Jun   25,   2015   at   2:34   PM
Subject: HR (CITY OF CAPE TOWN) PAY BACK MY MONEY

To: "Archie.Hearne@samwu.org.za"
<Archie.Hearne@samwu.org.za>, Sidney Flusk
<Sidney.Flusk@capetown.gov.za>, Patricia De Lille
<Patricia.DeLille@capetown.gov.za>, "Papikie@samwu.org.za"
<Papikie@samwu.org.za>, Mikel Khumalo
<mikel.khumalo@samwu.org.za>

*Cc: Goretti Francisco <Goretti.Francisco@capetown.gov.za>,
Edmund Jacobs <Edmund.Jacobs@capetown.gov.za>, Keith
Lakay <Keith.Lakay@capetown.gov.za>, Ninnie Steyn
<Ninnie.Steyn@capetown.gov.za>,*
"andre.timotheus@gmail.com" <andre.timotheus@gmail.com>,
"umcedi@gmail.com" <umcedi@gmail.com>,
"Lendy.Swartbooi@gmail.com" <Lendy.Swartbooi@gmail.com>

*Goretti its you again. PAY BACK MY
MONEY!!!*

*Firstly email my union Mr Archie Hearne or Sidney Flusk at
SAMWU office not me regarding my salary. You (the city of cape
town) have already deducted money from me and told me I will
not get it back again. Must I forward you my emails that you
stated it in black and white. I will not allow the city of cape town
to put my family through hell again. Its 21 years of democracy
and black people are still treated as slaves. PAY BACK MY*

MONEY. Black lives matter. Its because of the city of cape town I was on sick leave (depression)in the first place. SAMWU must stop racism in the western cape.

I am well aware that Christelle Lubbe (City of Cape Town) have caused this its called Promoting White Supremacy. The city of cape town is clearly promoting the Legacy of apartheid by taking a big portion of my salary. Just because I have been taking them to grievance Level 3 for promoting white supremacy, Racism, Victimization and Discrimination.

DISMANTLE WHITE SUPREMACY IN THE WESTERN CAPE!

No emails . PAY BACK MY MONEY

Lendy

(S

Grievance level 2

Forwarded message ----------
From: Xolani Diniso <Xolani.Diniso@capetown.gov.za>
Date: Tue, Apr 21, 2015 at 12:23 PM

Subject: *ENOUGH*   *IS*   *ENOUGH*

To: *Tania*   *Alcock-Smith*   *<Tania.Alcock-Smith@capetown.gov.za>,*   *Lendy*   *Thobejane <Lendy.Thobejane@capetown.gov.za>,* "*Lendy.Swartbooi@gmail.com*" *<Lendy.Swartbooi@gmail.com>*

Cc: Matt Stopka <Matt.Stopka@capetown.gov.za>, Christelle Lubbe   *<Christelle.Lubbe@capetown.gov.za>*

Good day all

i humbly apologise for responding so late regarding the minutes of the grievance that was reffer to level 2 by Mrs Thobejane. we were given 5 working days to respond if we want to escalate the grievance to level 3 or we satisfy with the desire outcome, to our suprise yesterday Mrs Thobejane was handed a charge sheet of 3 charges, all of these charges are taken on the list of grievance that she submitted long time ago. the union is taking the matter to level 3, because we cannot fold our arms when our member is being victimase by fighting for her rights not to be violeted by Mrs Lubbe. SAMWU leadership will be attending a meeting today at civic centre 14h30 with the city Mayor to talk about the issue of victimasation and discrimination in the workplace, we can attest to you that the issue of Mrs Thobejane will be on the top of the Agenda without fear or intimidation. ENOUGH IS ENOUGH Yours in struggle for condusive working place Xolani Diniso SAMWU (Health and Libraries Chairperson)

(T)From: Tania Alcock-Smith Sent: 20 April 2015 11:50 AM To: Lendy Thobejane; Lendy.Swartbooi@gmail.com Cc: Xolani Diniso; Christelle Lubbe; Matt Stopka; Denise.cleophas@imatucp.org.za Subject: RE: notes of grievance Level 2

Dear Ms Thobejane

Thank you for your e-mail.

As requested on Friday, attached is a scanned copy of the minutes of the level 2 grievance meeting held on 9 April 2015 that you had received and, after your telephonic discussion with your union representative (Mr Xolani Diniso), had signed for.

In our discussion, I indicated that you had 5 working days within which to consider the minutes. Thereafter you would complete the grievance form (attached as Annexure A) to indicate whether you are satisfied / not satisfied with the outcomes. If required, I would then submit the completed grievance form with all the supporting documentation to level 3.

In our discussion I further confirmed that the issue of transfer was discussed with line management. At this stage is there is no vacancy in a library meeting your criteria (i.e. a smaller library in a marginalised / disadvantaged community). Line management is however aware of possible retirements and resignations and has provided an undertaken to ensure that you are transferred by no later than 30 June 2015.

I understand that this morning (at ±8:59am) you had escalated the grievance to level 3. Please be advised that the grievance was returned to level 2 as there is no indication on the documentation submitted that it has been dealt with at level 2.

Regards,

Tania Alcock-Smith Support Manager Library & Information Services Ground Floor, 53 Berkley Rd, Maitland Tel: 021 400 5839 Fax: 086 632 0347 Cell: 084 350 7897 E-Mail: <u>tania.alcock-smith@capetown.gov.za</u>

(U)

From: Keith Lakay
Sent: 24 June 2015 01:50 PM To: Goretti Francisco Cc: Edmund Jacobs Subject: FW: EIC Service Request: 1200095555, Salary LC Thobejane 10046475

FYA and copy me in with your response.

Thanks

From: HR Service Desk
Sent: 24 June 2015 01:04 PM
To: Keith Lakay

Subject: EIC Service Request: 1200095555, Salary LC Thobejane 10046475

Good day

Kindly assist with this query please, LC Thobejane 10046475 would like to know why the is such a big difference in her salary please. her contact details are : 0796421675 and her land line 0219806160

Should you have any further queries, please contact us on (021)

400 3434 or email us at <u>hrservicedesk@capetown.gov.za</u> and have the above Service Request ID available

Regards,

HR Service Desk Team

(V)

Forwarded   message   ----------

From: Lendy   Swartbooi   <lendy.swartbooi@gmail.com>

Date: Sat,   Feb   20,   2016   at   12:06   PM

Subject: Bullying   at   work   does   not   stop

To: Achmat.Ebrahim@capetown.gov.za,   "lokiwe.   mtwazi" <lokiwe.mtwazi@capetown.gov.za>,

Patricia.DeLille@capetown.gov.za,   "mikel.   khumalo" <mikel.khumalo@samwu.org.za>,   Bernard   Joseph <bdjoseph3008@gmail.com>,   Yerushka   Chetty <yerushka@gmail.com>

Dear Mr Achmat Ebrahim

You are well informed I have exhausted all communication levels. From level one line manager , level 2 Director , Level 3 executive director.

I came late for work this morning for work because of mental sickness caused by the city. I was ask several times by Sisanda Mtyi librarian at eikendal library do storytelling during the week and she told me that its part of my job description. Even this morning have made it clear to her that Matt Stopka the Labour Relationship told me assistant librarians do not ran programs at the library.

The city have made sure I cannot email them. Therefore I ask her permission to buy data so that I can email the city from my cellphone. She refused. I told her I will alert my union she said go and email your union who fears the city.

The very same Sisanda provided the city with the wrong information and told the city I was crying by her. The city used that as evidence at CCMA. Ask Matt Stopka about the email.

When will city stop bullying and harrasssing me.

Matt Stopka said on record Lendy is not qualified to do storytelling in libraries at CCMA. Matt Stopka said its the job of librarians not assistant librarians.

A white woman committed a serious crime. She did not have a four year qualification in library science but did storytelling she has a degree in Police. She was employed as a librarian by the city. Ask Matt Stopka about a white woman Isabel Young a librarian at Ravensmead library that resign only after I exposed *the racism in the city. Ask Matt Stopka Isabel Young was at CCMA admit on record she does not have a degree in library science but she's a qualified policewoman.*

Matt Stopka must inform librarians what is my job description. This storytellingis add on to the unpleasant inviroment I have at work already.

A lot happened this morning. I will discuss further if give an opportunity to do so.

Khoisan   *descendants*

Lendy

Employed at eikendal library.

Dismissal: The matter to be continued at Halday Attorneys.